READING CULTURE
through
CATHOLIC EYES

READING CULTURE
through
CATHOLIC EYES

Fifty Writers, Thinkers, and Firebrands Who Challenge and Change Us

JAMES T. KEANE

ORBIS BOOKS
Maryknoll, New York 10545

Founded in 1970, Orbis Books endeavors to publish works that enlighten the mind, nourish the spirit, and challenge the conscience. The publishing arm of the Maryknoll Fathers and Brothers, Orbis seeks to explore the global dimensions of the Christian faith and mission, to invite dialogue with diverse cultures and religious traditions, and to serve the cause of reconciliation and peace. The books published reflect the views of their authors and do not represent the official position of the Maryknoll Society. To learn more about Orbis Books, please visit our website at www.orbisbooks.com.

Library of Congress Cataloging-in-Publication Data

Names: Keane, James T., author.
Title: Reading culture through Catholic eyes : 50 writers, thinkers, and firebrands who challenge and change us / James T. Keane.
Description: Maryknoll, NY : Orbis Books, [2024] | Summary: "Fifty varied voices reflect on their cultural, political, literary, and religious influence"—Provided by publisher.
Identifiers: LCCN 2024022812 (print) | LCCN 2024022813 (ebook) | ISBN 9781626985971 (trade paperback) | ISBN 9798888660423 (epub)
Subjects: LCSH: Essays. | Catholic authors. | Catholic Church--In literature. | Catholics in literature. | LCGFT: Essays.
Classification: LCC PN6142 .K43 2024 (print) | LCC PN6142 (ebook) | DDC 808—dc23/eng/20240802
LC record available at https://lccn.loc.gov/2024022812
LC ebook record available at https://lccn.loc.gov/2024022813

For Bob and Maureen

CONTENTS

FOREWORD

James Martin, S.J.

I have always loved libraries.
From the little elementary school library in the quiet suburb where I grew up through the many educational institutions life has brought me to and even in the many Jesuit communities I have called home over the past four decades, I have always found a particular welcome and place of rest and recreation in libraries. That includes the Ridge Park Elementary School library, where I pored over selections from Scholastic Books in my early years; the University of Pennsylvania's huge Van Pelt Library, where I spent college hours studying; the library of the Jesuit headquarters in Rome, with its centuries-old manuscripts and letters; the little William Jeanes Library, run by the Quakers, near my childhood home in Plymouth Meeting, Pennsylvania; and the smallest Jesuit community "free desk" near me in New York of just a few hundred books.

If you're a lover of the written word, you know what I mean. I owe God, my parents, and my many teachers over the years most of the credit for my life now as a priest and a writer, but some credit also goes to the book treasuries I discovered and enjoyed along the way.

When reading an early draft of James T. Keane's *Reading Culture through Catholic Eyes*, I was reminded of those many beloved places of edification and education, because it strikes me that he has composed a mini-library of sorts with this book. In almost every case, each of Jim's individual essays is an introduction to a much larger body of work—like going to a card catalog (for any young people reading this, that's how we looked things up at the library for, oh, a century or so) as a kid and finding not only the book you wanted but a dozen more by the same author or on the same subject. This is a book to read with a lot of Post-its by your side, or a pencil or pen in your hand, because you're going to mark a lot of pages with notes reminding yourself to learn more about the work of the writers, thinkers, and firebrands Jim explores.

When I first met Jim over twenty years ago, he was a new intern at *America*. (Readers of this book will not be surprised that his first article for *America* was a review of a book on Bob Dylan's use of Scripture in his songs.) We didn't have an office for him, or really even a private space to work. We set up him and the other intern—Matt Malone, S.J., who years later would become *America*'s editor in chief—at desks in the multiroom house library at America House, one that spanned half a dozen small rooms on the third floor. It meant that their desks were situated among floor-to-ceiling shelves filled with almost a century's worth of books. Some were academic texts, some religious devotionals, some fiction, some just the random stuff that past editors and Jesuit residents donated to the house. Every time I passed Jim's desk, I noticed he had his nose buried in one book or another. I finally asked him if he was working on a research project for the magazine.

"Sort of," he said. "I'm also off on the world's wildest literary tangent." He pointed to the book he was reading by the Catholic theologian Romano Guardini.

For the record, he did complete his actual research project—an informal history of the magazine—before his internship ended. But his love for diverse sources and his curiosity around making connections as well as his love for those firebrand outlier voices gave a foretaste of things to come.

Some of these authors in this book I knew already—in fact, I think in a couple of cases I might have been the one to introduce Jim to their work. But even for the authors with whom I was familiar, I was impressed: Jim has a knack for something many writers take a lifetime to learn—he can write a succinct introduction to an author or a subject while also providing readers all the pertinent (or fascinating) information they need. (He is, as I often tell people, the very best writer on our staff.) I was surprised to realize that most of the entries in this collection are less than one thousand words. How does one sum up Thomas Merton or Dorothy Day or Mary Karr or Sigrid Undset in nine hundred words? As someone whose last book approached four hundred pages, I can tell you: it ain't easy.

That was for the authors I knew. Jim's collection, drawn mostly from his weekly columns for *America*, also introduced me to a cornucopia of new authors. I have long known the name Christopher Lasch; I had no idea what he had written. Ditto for Kirstin Valdez Quade, Theophilus Lewis, William Lynch, and Sally Rooney. Then there are the writers whose work I thought I knew inside and out—people like Mary Gordon, Ron Hansen, Alice McDermott, Toni Morrison, and more—whose lives and writing careers turned out to have many more twists and turns than I had thought. This book is full of such moments.

Readers will also note right off the bat that Jim has assembled a somewhat eclectic menagerie of authors here, not all of whom easily attach to the same through-line. Forget Athens and Jerusalem. What does Mike Davis have to do with Fulton Sheen? Where is the connection between John Courtney Murray and Martin Amis? I think the easiest answer is this: Jim's writing in this book is both Catholic and catholic. Jim's own literary and religious appetites are a bit more omnivorous than most, and so that through-line can be hidden to some of us. But if you recognize that every one of us exists under a big tent—what was it Pope Francis's synod encouraged us all to do? "Enlarge the space of your tent"?—then you begin to understand the wider connections. They make more sense. The number one reason every single author appears here is that they obviously had some positive (or valuable) impact on Jim's own faith and life, his Catholic/catholic way of reading the world. And what more primal instinct is there for a writer but that desire to share such good news with others?

Maybe his wide-ranging reads and curiosity come in part from Jim's father, who was, believe it or not, a television comedy writer, someone who wrote jokes for people like Johnny Carson, Bob Hope, Dean Martin, and more. He also contributed jokes to a few presidential and senatorial candidates over the years (and a few priests looking for some writing help as well). That gift for the unexpected quip, the clever aside, the on-point insight that makes you laugh before you even realize what you're laughing at, was passed down from father to son and is evidenced throughout these pages. Whatever else this book is, it is also pretty funny. Just like Jim, whose humor and wit are well known and well appreciated in the office and by *America*'s readers.

There are at least two very profitable ways to read this book. The first—to which the book's structure lends itself—

is to read about one author a day. Morning, night, whenever. Just pick a time to be intrigued and possibly educated a bit about an author, thinker, or firebrand you love—or one you never heard of. The second is to lose yourself in the worlds the book opens the door to—to keep reading until there's just too much information, too many funny anecdotes, too many intriguing asides for your brain to process. Then after your brain rests and processes the book, return to it again.

It has been a real pleasure to work with Jim so often over the years. In addition to our time together at *America*, he also edited a book of my own collected writings for Orbis Books. I was surprised when I read his preface to that book how deeply he had read into books and articles I had written years before but found minor or lacking in substance; somehow he was able to conjure up meaning and connections where I had found little or none. He is someone I trust to read early drafts of my own new work (he actually coined the title for *Between Heaven and Mirth*). In that sense, it is an honor to return the favor and read this erudite, intriguing, and often charming book of stories, ideas, change-makers, and C/catholic thought.

Let me reemphasize this one thing: Jim is a terrific writer. I've long admired his style: lucid, smooth, clever, provocative, and most of all inviting. So in addition to reading *about* great authors and thinkers, you'll be guided through their work by another one.

Enjoy this book. Add it to your library. Treat it like its own little library, and enjoy the education, challenge, edification, and joy of reading Jim's musings on so many of our greatest writers, thinkers, and firebrands.

INTRODUCTION

I grew up in a house filled with people and full of books. The people were my parents and their eight children, as well as the countless friends, relatives, neighbors, classmates, and more who found an open door to our home. The books in our home were from everywhere.

Some were our parents' textbooks from the 1950s and 1960s, including a vast number of works of fiction; some were from their children's high school and college classes; some were tomes both new and used bought at bookstores; some were part of my father's always-growing collection of books by and about Thomas More and the Renaissance; and some, of course, were page-turners by Tom Clancy and Robert Ludlum and Michael Crichton and Sue Grafton or books about dinosaurs. (To the deep-thinker-reader, don't knock it till you've tried it; a Tom Clancy novel makes an excellent *amuse-bouche*.)

Despite my father's occupation as a television comedy writer, my parents were not big fans of television—to this day, I sometimes notice visitors to my mother's home looking around the living room, disconcerted: *where the hell is the TV?* And of course there was no such thing as social media or the internet in those days. We were all voracious readers in my family, something I never really noticed myself until I was home from college one summer and a buddy said, "WTF, Keane, I stopped by your parents' house and there were five people in the living room reading in silence."

One night when I was a preteen, I reached over to a bookshelf in our living room and pulled out a slim paperback novel: *Mr. Blue*. Who knows why I grabbed it; perhaps the slight little thing looked out of place among the huskier tomes surrounding it and slowly crushing it to pulp. I opened it and took a look. From across the room, my father perked up. "*Mr. Blue!* What a book! Had a huge impact on me." Since truthfully the only book that had occasioned a similar feeling in me up to that point had been Clancy's *Red Storm Rising*, I figured I would give Myles Connolly's 1928 classic a read.

Truth be told, I didn't really understand *Mr. Blue*. I don't think I had much of a sense of what it was about until after I read *The Great Gatsby*, which had been published three years before *Mr. Blue* and was still a staple of high school curricula in the early 1990s. But it got me started on a quixotic path that soon included Chinua Achebe's *Things Fall Apart*, Walter Miller Jr.'s *A Canticle for Leibowitz*, and J. F. Powers's *Look How the Fish Live* (all of which were also to be found on a shelf somewhere in that house in Burbank). Did I read them more than I read *Sabre Jet Ace* or *Jurassic Park*? Certainly not, but it was a start.

"There is always one moment in childhood when the door opens and lets the future in," Graham Greene wrote in *The Power and the Glory*, a line that I love (and one I think John Irving has used in half a dozen novels). While I can't identify one single moment when that happened, a series of reading moments in that Burbank living room grew into my own journey as a writer.

Years later, I took a class in college somewhat misleadingly titled "Philosophy and Fiction," because in all fairness it was a course on Catholic novels. We read Graham Greene,

Muriel Spark, Walker Percy, Flannery O'Connor, Shusaku Endo, Evelyn Waugh, J. F. Powers, and more. (Yes, it was mostly white male authors.) That class gave me more insight into the worlds of pedagogy and reading for enjoyment—and into the notion that it is possible to communicate some of the great truths (and most of the great struggles) of human existence through the imagining of a scene. Years later when I was introduced more fully to Ignatian spirituality, I found a similar idea sketched out in St. Ignatius's notion of "contemplation of place," imagining oneself inside a Gospel story.

After that class ended, I read everything J. F. Powers wrote, including his second novel, *Wheat That Springeth Green*. I consumed as much Graham Greene as I could before the sheer angst of so many of his characters wore me out. I read more Flannery O'Connor, even those stories I didn't (and don't) understand. And they led me to authors who would perhaps be appalled to be included in a catalog of Catholic writers, like John Irving. Is *The World according to Garp* a great Catholic novel? Assuredly not. But it is a great, great novel.

Years later, while working at *America* as an associate editor and a Jesuit seminarian, I began to meet some of the writers who occupied places of great honor in my brain: fiction writers like Ron Hansen, Mary Gordon, Alice McDermott, Tobias Wolff, David Plante; spiritual writers like James Martin, S.J., Robert Ellsberg, Daniel Berrigan, S.J., and Anne Lamott; theologians like Roger Haight, Beth Johnson, James Alison, Avery Dulles, and many more.

Around that time, Father Mark Massa, a Jesuit priest at Fordham University, offered me the chance to teach a course on "American Catholic Novels" in the Curran Center for American Catholic Studies. Father Massa was something of a wizard when it came to getting students into desks, and so I soon found myself teaching a course that was cross-listed for credit with Fordham majors like Theology, English, American Studies, and History. After a disastrous first class in which my lecture turned out to be thirteen minutes long, I settled into the course and found I loved it—loved the students, loved the material, loved the way a writer even from prior centuries could still touch the postmodern heart and soul. After a couple of semesters, Father Massa asked me to change the topic to "Catholic Novels Worldwide" so we could make it qualify for the students' Globalism course requirement, which widened my reading directions and opened my interests even more.

When in graduate school for theology in Berkeley a few years later, I taught similar courses through the St. Ignatius Institute at the University of San Francisco. The director of the institute, Father Sean Michaelson, S.J., made a deal with me: if I taught a Capstone course on "Spiritual Memoir" in the spring, in the fall I could teach the class I had been campaigning for since day one: "The Poetics of Bob Dylan." The Dylan class was something of a disaster (I know, shocking), but the course on spiritual memoirs expanded my literary interests significantly. The students had no time for bullshit or false piety—both of which, ahem, sometimes find their way into spiritual memoirs, and novels too. The students in the class possessed lively imaginations and a lot of insight.

After I left the Jesuits in 2012, I spent five years working at Orbis Books as an acquisitions editor and editing the work of some of the world's foremost Catholic theologians (and many fiery social activists and cultural critics as well). If there is a more polite way to describe it, I will take it, but I was a pig in [a wallow]. I returned to *America* in 2017 as the literary editor, and soon began writing a weekly email newsletter on the magazine's book reviews and archival material, a role that eventually morphed into a weekly column on the same.

Like most writers and layabouts, I do better with a deadline. It turns out "every Tuesday afternoon" is a rather powerful goad to one's creativity and production. So, too, is Covid time, when we were all reading more (or clicking more, whatever), and one day I looked up and I had something like 150 columns under my belt. And after years of writing the column and getting reader feedback, I discovered that I wasn't alone in valuing literature for the way it informed my lived experience, my understanding of my Catholic identity, or simply my spiritual sensibilities.

This book was born from that project. I hope it works as an invitation to similar journeys for the reader. I expanded some of the columns, redacted others, and simply abandoned a lot of them because no one but me wants to read about C. J. McNaspy's corn cob pipe and his plans for a chapel on the moon. I took a lot of joy from writing this book—with some failed work along the way—and I am grateful for the ongoing learning that has kept me blessed and busy for so many years.

I am grateful to *America* for permission to use my columns in this book and thankful for the many editors who helped with their original publication in the magazine—most especially several generations of literary assistants who put up with my idiosyncrasies while also deleting my sidelong attacks on Mary Oliver and the San Francisco Giants. Angelo Canta, Colleen Dulle, Emma Winters, Sarah Vincent, Jill Rice, and Christine Lenahan all deserve extensive time off in purgatory for their patience and labor.

So, too, am I grateful for everyone at Orbis Books, especially Lil Copan, Robert Ellsberg, Bernadette Price, and Maria Angelini—who should also be forgiven for shouting at me about deadlines and misspellings. I consider it a great honor to be published with Orbis, not least because it keeps me in the company of so many writers and theologians I admire.

James T. Keane

1

Myles Connolly
"Why Are All of Us Here and Not Blue?"

Why are American Catholic writers so boring? I'm not asking the above question, mind you. Just repeating it. Myles Connolly asked and answered it in something of a jeremiad written eight decades ago—and yet some of his criticisms remain relevant today.

Never heard of Myles Connolly? He achieved some minor literary success with his simple yet beguiling 1928 novel, *Mr. Blue*, but his bread and butter was Hollywood. His Boston friend Joseph Kennedy (yes, that Joe Kennedy) first hired him to work as a screenwriter at Kennedy's fledgling movie studio, and Connolly wrote a number of screenplays before eventually moving into a producer's role. His writing credits—*The Right to Romance* (1933), *Palm Springs* (1936), *Youth Takes a Fling* (1938), *Music for Millions* (1944), and *Hans Christian Andersen* (1952)—are less impressive than his uncredited contributions to Frank Capra's classic films *Mr. Smith Goes to Washington* and *It's a Wonderful Life*.

Capra and Connolly were close friends and frequent collaborators, and Connolly served as godfather to three of Capra's children. Capra once described Connolly as a "hulking, 230-pound, six-three, black-hair, blue-eyed gum-

1

chewing Irishman with the mien of a dyspeptic water buffalo." Connolly was also a devout Catholic who had once
served as editor of *Columbia*, the official magazine of the
Knights of Columbus.

He wrote for Catholic journals frequently in the 1930s,
including a long essay for *America* on American Catholic
writers in 1935. The essay started politely enough, but once
Connolly got warmed up, the "dyspeptic water buffalo"
made its appearance.

"First of all, I would like to say there is no paucity of
American Catholic writers appearing in contemporary print.
The amount of lead, ink, typewriter ribbon, paper, and print
mutilated by them in the course of a year would fill—and
should—a pit slightly larger, I imagine, than the Grand Can-
yon," he wrote. "The beautifully pitiful complaint that there
are too few of them is immediately false to any honest man
who has sat behind a Catholic editor's desk and tried to read
the exchanges."

Despite the abundance of these writers, he wrote, few were
readable:

> Together, they constitute a voice that is about as
> effectual as the crackling of a frosted telephone wire
> in the depth of night. Why? Because they are dull. I
> can't read them, and few others can, for the simple
> reason that I and the others do not care to be bored.

He didn't mince words for the next few paragraphs. "A
good-tempered argument sometimes—not often—achieves
results. A bad-tempered argument, never," Connolly continued, in a description that presciently describes "Catholic
Twitter" to a T. "But so great is the American Catholic love of
argument and belief in the efficacy of argument—the more

vicious the better—that the American Catholic writer flings off his coat at the first cry and lays about him. The ghosts are triumphantly laid, and the straw men destroyed, with a vigor, and often a viciousness, that gives the writer huge satisfaction—and few else except, perhaps, the members of his immediate family."

Why this cantankerousness? "Ordinarily, it springs from that extraordinary sense of inferiority which prompts bragging that someone like Babe Ruth is a Catholic and, at practically the same moment, resenting any criticism as unjust and malevolent. It comes from a weakness that knows no calm, no subtlety, no ingenuity, a weakness that defends itself with an obvious everlasting chip on the shoulder," Connolly wrote. "Less ordinarily, it comes from ignorance, or, I might say, guilelessness. It has never occurred to the writer that there is craft—even craftiness—in effective writing. Writing, to such a writer, is a physical exercise resembling cheering or, rather, booing, at a football game."

Why this state of affairs? Because the American Catholic writer "has all his life been clouded with the traditional—and occasionally wise—suspicion of anything interesting. He has similarly been deeply impressed with the noble belief that truth, however stupidly stated, eventually triumphs," Connolly continued. Such a writer "takes to platitudes like pigeons to peanuts. He hesitates to try to be interesting. He shies from being amusing. He shuns satire. He suspects passion. He shuts his eyes at ecstasy. He is afraid of tenderness. And he flees from laughter."

Ouch! In the words of another generation, *way harsh.*

"I have not the space here to suggest the necessity of a thoughtful, considered, even artistic approach to popular Catholic writing," Connolly wrote. "I may, however, suggest that a writer achieves power only by rigid individual discipline and preparation; that he must discover and hew to a standard of taste; that he must beware of movements and committees; that, ultimately, in his own temperament lies the key to his method and distinction; that, in a word, in the silence of his own soul he must work out his style, which is his salvation."

Connolly wasn't always so grumpy. *Mr. Blue*, for example, is a gentle and simply told tale of a modern-day St. Francis of Assisi wandering the streets of New York—as well as an eerie prefiguring of Dorothy Day and the Catholic Worker. Its eponymous main character abandons his wealth and ambition to live a life of unhoused simplicity, an anti-Gatsby in every way (Fitzgerald's famous novel had been published in 1925, three years before). Written at the very height of the Roaring Twenties, *Mr. Blue* lamented the decline of religion, spiritual commitment, and friendship in modern life and suggested that a kind of moral bankruptcy was hidden behind the booming economy—an economy that would collapse almost entirely just a year later.

Why does Mr. Blue sound like he's quoting Pope Francis's encyclical *Fratelli Tutti*? They might be more simpatico than you think: in her preface to the 2016 reissue of *Mr. Blue* (which had gone out of print), Connolly's daughter Mary Connolly Breiner suggested that Pope Francis would love the character of Mr. Blue and described them as "true brothers in spirit."

Cardinal Timothy Dolan of New York once called *Mr. Blue* one of his favorite novels, and John Sexton, the president emeritus of New York University, once said in an interview that "the goal for all of us is to be like Mr. Blue."

In 2016, Paul Almonte wrote that "*Mr. Blue*'s relevance

endures because of its call to look deeply inward and compassionately outward, to question oneself while embracing the plight, worries, and needs of others. Blue's life—his words, actions and his death—invite us to consider our own place and role among the 'new masses.' To read the novel seriously is to embrace the question the narrator asks at the end: 'why are all of us here and not Blue?'"

2

XAVIER RYNNE
Holy Gossip

When the church historian Massimo Faggioli came to do research in New York City in June 2023, he uncovered a treasure trove of "poems on postcards" from the 1960s by John Cogley, former managing editor of *Commonweal* and later the religion editor of the *New York Times*. One, "Literary Intelligence," offered quick and pithy IDs of many prominent writers ("Hans Küng is only thirty-five" / "Upton Sinclair is quite alive"), but finished with a question on everyone's mind during the Second Vatican Council:

> I know their habits, their next of kin
> But who the hell is Xavier Rynne?

Cogley wasn't the only one asking. Writing in the *New Yorker*, the mysterious Xavier Rynne was spilling all the tea during Vatican II. His "Letter from Vatican City" ran from 1962 through 1965, and offered an unvarnished, mostly uncensored take on the internal operations of the council. His columns played a major role in the Catholic public perception of the council—including the description of opposing camps of traditionalist bishops and reformer bishops that became a major takeaway for many readers, Catholic and not.

But no one could quite figure out who the author really was. He was obviously an American, but he was trading gossip with Italian reporters and recording observations made in Vatican stairwells like the wiliest of Romans.

So who was he, really? Francis X. Murphy, an American Redemptorist priest serving as a theological adviser (a *peritus*) to a Redemptorist bishop at the council, Bishop Aloysius Willinger. Murphy had written for American Catholic periodicals for years, and leading up to the council his writing drew the attention of Robert Giroux, legendary editor from Farrar, Straus & Giroux, who approached the *New Yorker* editor William Shawn about running Murphy as a columnist in the magazine.

Because much of Murphy's reporting on the Vatican was on sensitive and nonpublic matters—often the ecclesial gossip he overheard in elevators and in meals with reporters and other theological advisers—he and Shawn decided a pseudonym would be best, and formed this from his middle name and his mother's maiden name.

The *New Yorker* scored quite a coup with Rynne's columns, especially as it became clear that the Vatican Curia was dominated by traditionalist bishops and cardinals who opposed many of the council reforms but were eventually sidelined by the sheer number of bishops from around the world seeking reform—and by the latter's theological experts, many of whom became household names for Catholics in the years after the council: Rahner, Ratzinger, Congar, Schillebeeckx, Küng, de Lubac, and more.

Some bishops and Vatican officials attempted to suss out the true author behind Xavier Rynne during the council, and he later claimed that he had been called in at one point by the secretary of the Congregation for the Doctrine of the Faith after he had described the man, an Italian archbishop, in a column as "a strange personality who has few friends and sees heresy everywhere."

Murphy's contract with the *New Yorker* wasn't exclusive, and he continued writing about the council under his true name for various church outlets, including a March 9, 1963, essay in *America*, "Vatican II: Early Appraisal." His identity eventually became something of an open secret—his writing style had much of the same "here is the inside scoop" flavor as his work for the *New Yorker*—but for decades he refused to admit it publicly. In the years after the council, editors took to delicately describing Rynne in articles as someone "well-accredited in the field of Roman documents" and "a long-term observer of the Roman scene." When he reported on the 1985 Extraordinary Synod of Bishops in Rome, *America* settled on the following author ID:

> Francis X. Murphy, C.Ss.R., is a church historian who supervised contributions to the *New Catholic Encyclopedia* and is thought, perhaps inaccurately, to be Xavier Rynne, pseudonymous author of *Letters from Vatican City* written during the Second Vatican Council.

Murphy served for years after the council in Rome and in the United States as a university professor and seminary rector. He died in 2002 at the age of eighty-seven. Four years earlier, in 1998, Murphy had finally confirmed to a Religion News Service reporter that he was the real Xavier Rynne.

Why did Murphy choose finally to reveal his true identity? "I was afraid that if I went to my grave without making it known," he told the reporter, "the damned Jesuits would have claimed it was one of theirs and the Redemptorists would have been just as happy."

3

MARTIN AMIS
Omnivorous Wordsmith

Martin Amis was an acquired taste.

It is in fact easy today to look at the corpus of work by the British writer, who died of cancer in 2023 at the age of seventy-three in Florida, and find a lot of it distasteful. The novels, the essays, and the countless articles have not all aged well. Outrageous, witty, insightful, quick on his feet, omnivorous in his appetite for prey, Amis also comes across often enough as an arrogant, entitled, sexist, classist bully who sought out offense rather than dealing with controversies as they came. It is not impossible to imagine that if he were in his prime today, he would have a drink too many at a book launch and announce that Donald Trump was misunderstood.

At the same time, writers sometimes get a pass that the rest of us don't—why else would anyone still be reading Norman Mailer or Philip Roth—and while I can see all of the above about Amis is true, I also greatly admired and enjoyed his writing. A. O. Scott noted upon Amis's death that Amis had a particular appeal to members of Generation X (whom Amis, charming to the last, called "the crap generation"), and a cursory look at the tributes to him offers anecdotal

confirmation. If nothing else, his famous father, the writer
Kingsley Amis (himself hilarious and cruel, and *Lucky Jim*
still slaps), found far more favor with high-brow writers and
editors than his son ever did.

While Amis's nonfiction is to my mind the crown jewel of
his collection—I have never been in a dentist's chair and not
recalled his harrowing account in his memoir *Experience* of
having all his teeth pulled—I first encountered him through
his 1984 novel, *Money: A Suicide Note.* Living in Philadelphia
in the late 1990s, I walked on my way from work every day
past an anarchist bookstore on South Street, The Wooden
Shoe. (It's still there, though the rest of South Street became
Disneyfied many years ago.) I would buy the *Nation* there,
mostly for the writing of Amis's boon companion and fellow literary bad boy, Christopher Hitchens, still a velveteen
Marxist in those days.

A friend leaving Philadelphia to begin an M.F.A. program
went to The Wooden Shoe with me and found *Money* in its
stacks (presumably it was there because of the connection
with Hitchens) and bought it for me as a farewell present.
"You'll love it," she said. "It's hilarious and so accurate."

Fifty pages in, I was somewhat taken aback. The first-person
tale of a British *enfant terrible* crashing around Manhattan
amid vague plans to make a movie, it was an unrelenting
barrage of boastful sexual conquests, boozy lunches, lengthy
descriptions of pornographic theaters, and no end of frenzied
consumption, and struck me as exactly the sort of book my
friend would hate. I told her as much on the phone. And she
responded in a way that would make Amis proud: stop being
a ninny; grow up, and finish the book.

She was right. By the time I reached the end of the novel,
I recognized that the debauched character of John Self was

more than just a British version of a Jay McInerny protagonist or Bret Easton Ellis antihero: he was a warning.

Money is a laugh a minute and a sensory roller coaster, but it is also at the end a profound if somewhat exhausting parable: *here is what happens when you deny yourself nothing.* Amis himself quite obviously knew well what his fictional alter ego John Self figured out, and I'm not sure that he didn't have even more fun than John Self did while learning it; but *Money* is ultimately a fantastic and deeply insightful novel. Who knew that, deep down, Martin Amis was a moralist?

There were plenty of other novels before and after, including *London Fields* and *The Information*, and in 2020 Amis published *Inside Story*, an autobiographical novel full of his typical snark and score-settling but also touching in its relating of how many friends and heroes the septuagenarian had lost by then, including Hitchens from the same esophageal cancer that would kill Amis himself. And, of course, there were the hundreds of thousands of pages of nonfiction.

His 2001 collection *The War against Cliché* offers his best writing and his worst, and somehow enraged critics even though everything in it had already been published, some as much as three decades earlier. Amis's enemies had enemies when he was at his peak, and his savage wit and libertine antics earned him a nickname he probably wished he had invented himself: "Smarty Anus." The *New York Times* once described him as an avatar of "the new unpleasantness," writing that "his voice stands out discordantly from the rest like a boom box at a harpsichord recital." Along with Hitchens, Salman Rushdie, Ian McEwan, and James Fenton, he became a kind of icon of postcolonial British literature, witnesses to the dying of the empire and a culture deciding what came next.

Americans who read him might be surprised to hear that, because he strikes a lot of readers as more American than British: it was the shoulders of Saul Bellow and Vladimir Nabokov that Amis seemed to imagine himself standing on, after all, not those of his famous father. Like Hitchens and Rushdie, he existed in multiple cultures as an always recognizable voice, one not easily imitated. In a *New Yorker* tribute to Amis, McEwan recalled Amis's letter years ago to *Private Eye* (the magazine that gave him the aforementioned nickname) when someone had faked a letter to the editor in Amis's name. "I don't write like that," Amis began. "I write like this."

I dug out my old copy of *Money* after hearing of Smarty Anus's death and reread it. Still scabrously funny. Still exhausting. Still an acquired taste. And yet still a work of art. "Sometimes I feel that life is passing me by, not slowly either, but with ropes of steam and spark-spattered wheels and a hoarse roar of power or terror," says John Self. "It's passing, yet I'm the one who's doing all the moving. I'm not the station, I'm not the stop: I'm the train. I'm the train."

That was Martin Amis. Not the station, not the stop. The train.

4

John Moffitt
J. D. Salinger's Pen Pal

A symposium in April 2023 sponsored by the Free Library of Philadelphia marked the occasion of the 130th anniversary of the arrival in the United States of Swami Vivekananda, a young Hindu monk from Kolkata who toured the country and spoke at the 1893 Parliament of World Religions in Chicago, Illinois. Swami Vivekananda, a devotee of the Indian Hindu spiritual leader Sri Ramakrishna, gave many Americans their introduction to Hinduism and some of its practices (including yoga), and historians often mark Vivekananda's speeches in Chicago as the beginning of American interest in that faith tradition long before immigration from India and East Asia made it more common in the United States.

In Western literary circles Vivekananda became a sensation. William James invited him to speak at Harvard; Gertrude Stein and Leo Tolstoy numbered among his fans, with the latter calling him "the most brilliant wise man" and arguing that "it is doubtful in this age that another man has ever risen above this selfless, spiritual meditation." In later decades, everyone from Carl Jung to Joseph Campbell to Nikola Tesla to Henry Miller to Christopher Isherwood to Aldous Huxley were enthusiasts of the teachings of Vivekananda.

Among Vivekananda's disciples was John Moffitt, who spent over twenty-five years as a member of a Hindu monastic order and lived at the Ramakrishna-Vivekananda Center in New York City. (He records his story in the 1972 book, *Journey to Gorakhpur: An Encounter with Christ beyond Christianity,* on the kinship between Hindu and Christian beliefs.) Moffitt, known in those days as Swami Atmaghanananda, was only the sixth Westerner to be granted the title of swami, an honor that usually followed an apprenticeship of between five and fifteen years, and he carried on a prodigious correspondence with others interested in the Vedanta Hindu philosophical tradition specifically and spirituality in general.

Moffitt eventually converted to Catholicism in 1963. He served as poetry editor of *America* from 1963 until a month before his death from cancer in 1987, one of the first lay people to serve as an editor at the Jesuit magazine. He was also a pioneer of working from home, since he lived in a small town in West Virginia for most of his tenure. An accomplished poet, he published five collections of verse and saw his work appear in the *Atlantic,* the *Saturday Review,* and the *New Yorker.*

No historian should look to *America*—or, indeed, any Catholic publication—in the first half of the twentieth century for any sense of American interest in Hinduism, as it was rarely mentioned—and sometimes negatively if so, as in a 1931 *America* review of the book *Hinduism Invades America.* (Why is someone always invading America?) Moffitt, however, was that *rara avis,* a Catholic convert who did not reject the spiritual insights or wisdom of his former tradition.

"It is clear that Moffitt carefully looked at and listened to what was around him so that no false ego of his would usurp a deeper self," wrote the scholar Patrick Samway, S.J., in a 1993 remembrance of Moffitt. "He believed, moreover, in the eloquence of nature, and felt that his task as a poet was not to commit the pathetic fallacy of imposing feelings or emotions on an object beyond what the object and one's relationship with the object warranted. Like Gerard Manley Hopkins, someone who clearly influenced his poetry, Moffitt felt that the poet not only participates in the divinity but sees the world as a manifestation of the fullness of the Godhead."

One such literary acquaintance was a fellow devotee of Sri Ramakrishna and Swami Vivekananda, a writer Moffitt addressed simply as "Jerry," and they corresponded off and on from 1953 until 1965. It was J. D. Salinger, whose 1951 novel, *The Catcher in the Rye,* had propelled him to literary fame and who regularly published short stories in the *New Yorker* in the years following.

In one 1956 letter, Salinger complained to Moffitt about "his own relationship with another Hindu monk, most likely Moffitt's spiritual guide, Swami Nikhilananda. Salinger felt that Swami Nikhilananda had considered him outside the fold, thus putting a strain on their relationship," Samway reported. "But perhaps the feeling came from Salinger's own sense of impudence, a facet of his personality that he admitted seemed to be growing each year. Salinger believed that the only way to deal with this situation was to write himself out of his dilemmas." Salinger later gave Nikhilananda an inscribed copy of *Franny and Zooey,* confiding that he had left a trail of clues about the Vedanta philosophical tradition in the book.

The letters between Moffitt and Salinger offer some tantalizing literary tidbits as well. In one dated February 15, 1953, Salinger mentions that he made the title character in his short story "Teddy" (published in the *New Yorker* on January 31,

1953) slightly cross-eyed because Sri Ramakrishna considered the condition to be an unfavorable spiritual sign. Salinger also wrote that "the story mixed Vedanta, Zen Buddhism, Taoism, and perhaps other religions." In his last published work, the 1965 short story "Hapworth 16, 1924," Salinger's alter ego Seymour recommends two of Swami Vivekananda's books to his parents:

> Raja-Yoga and Bhakti-Yoga, two heartrending, handy, quite tiny volumes, perfect for the pockets of any average, mobile boy our age, by Vivekananda of India. He is one of the most exciting, original and best equipped giants of this century I have ever run into; my personal sympathy for him will never be outgrown or exhausted as long as I live, mark my words; I would easily give ten years of my life, possibly more, if I could have shaken his hand or at least said a brisk, respectful hello to him on some busy street in Calcutta or elsewhere.

While Salinger kept up a correspondence with Nikhilananda for many years, Moffitt felt Salinger's own letters tended to focus on interest in Hinduism, and he lost much of his interest in writing to Moffitt once Moffitt left the monastic community. However, in the years following his conversion to Catholicism, as Moffitt wrote and lectured frequently on Hinduism and Christianity, he developed another literary correspondence, this time with Thomas Merton.

Moffitt's letters—like his prose and poetry—give off a whiff of the vexed wanderer even when one reads them today, at a half-century's distance. But it was not a solitary journey, nor one without its landmarks. Would that we all had such interesting spiritual journeys and friends on our life's journey.

5

JOHN MOFFITT
(AND THOMAS MERTON)
Death in Bangkok

John Moffitt, the Catholic writer, editor, and poet who was a pen pal of J. D. Salinger (see the previous chapter), had another famous interlocutor, Thomas Merton, whom Moffitt met at a conference on monasticism outside Bangkok in December 1968—the conference where Merton died.

The two had never met in person before, though their youthful interests in religion have a curious point of connection. In his autobiography, *The Seven Storey Mountain*, Merton traced his interest in religion to reading Aldous Huxley's *Ends and Means*, a collection of essays on religion, ethics, and the nature of the universe. Huxley was among the many literary and cultural luminaries to take an interest in Swami Vivekananda's teachings, and he eventually became associated with the Vedanta Society of Southern California, even writing the introduction to an English translation of *The Gospel of Sri Ramakrishna*. The book's Bengali translator, Swami Nikhilananda, served as spiritual guide to both J. D. Salinger and John Moffitt. Credited with rendering Ramakrishna's mystic hymns into free verse was (you guessed it) John Moffitt.

Moffitt, as an accomplished poet with several collections to his name, was best known for the poem "To Look at Any Thing," from his 1962 book *The Living Seed*. Because of his rare status as a Western Christian steeped in Eastern monasticism after his 1963 conversion to Catholicism, he was invited to the December 1968 Meeting of Monastic Superiors in the Far East. The conference "brought together for the first time responsible representatives of all the monastic orders in the Far East under the Benedictine rule," Moffitt wrote in a 1969 article. The meeting also included specialists on "several of the non-Christian monasticisms of the East" as well as other men and women religious, with almost seventy in all in attendance. Presiding over the conference was Dom Rembert Weakland, O.S.B., the then–abbot primate of the Benedictine order.

On the morning of December 10, Merton spoke to the conference, a talk some recalled as disappointing. Two days earlier Merton and Moffitt met. Upon meeting him, Moffitt said, "There seemed no need of getting acquainted with Thomas Merton; it was as if one had known him always."

Because the two shared a four-room bungalow with two other participants, "there were many opportunities for exchanges of ideas," Moffitt later reflected. "Though I felt that his faith was unshakably serene, and sensed no desire on his part for any change in his way of life, I was nevertheless aware of a felt need in him for fuller intellectual satisfaction—for a larger formula, perhaps, that would enable him to include more of what felt was valid 'outside' the explicit Christian tradition."

The next night, December 9, Merton said something to Moffitt that would find its way into almost every later biography of Merton: "After the meeting broke up, we were again conversing, this time about Hinduism and Zen," Moffitt wrote, "when Fr. Merton exclaimed with unfeigned enthusiasm: 'Zen and Christianity are the future!'"

The next afternoon, Moffitt went on a sightseeing trip with some other monks. Returning home at 5 p.m., he was told Merton was dead—the result of a heart attack, possibly caused by electrocution from a faulty electric fan. "What really caused Fr. Merton's death will probably never be known," Moffitt wrote. "As Dom Weakland said to me, 'There is often something inexplicable about the death of great men. Perhaps we should just accept it as a mystery.'"

Moffitt was asked to move to other quarters. "When I arrived at the cottage to remove my belongings from my room, which was just above Fr. Merton's, Dom Rembert was seated outside, waiting for the police to arrive," Moffitt remembered. "They were slow in coming. As I passed by the open door, I could see Fr. Merton's body lying where it had originally fallen, with a dark red burn down his right side. All night, by turns, monks kept vigil by his bed."

The participants held a Requiem Mass for Merton the next morning. "The occasion was a moving one, but not at all sad," Moffitt wrote. "All the delegates felt that by this unexpected happening the conference had been given far greater depth—as one Indian delegate wrote to me afterward, it was 'sealed with the blood of Thomas Merton.'"

In January of 1970, an edited collection of the proceedings of the conference was published as *A New Charter for Monasticism*, with Moffitt serving as editor. Four years after Merton's death, Moffitt published a poem in honor of Merton, "By His Death":

In Memoriam: Thomas Merton
December 10, 1968

> By his death we are not diminished.
> He has entered
> into the space of thought,
> he walks on the light
> and serves where he serves.
> In his death
> surely we have no cause for dismay,
> being not diminished.
> When, in this little after hour,
> death sounds our summons,
> we too shall walk on the light
> if our cup is rinsed,
> and serve where we serve,
> with him in our Lord
> joined in perpetual act of creating.
> By his death and ours
> surely we are increased,
> we are not diminished.

6

Dorothy Day
Reluctant Saint

On December 8, 2021, in St. Patrick's Cathedral, Cardinal Timothy Dolan presided at a Mass to commemorate the advancement to Rome of Dorothy Day's cause for canonization.

Though she was famously reticent to describe herself as one ("Don't call me a saint," she once said, "I don't want to be dismissed that easily"), a saint is how many remember Dorothy Day today, even if it takes some time for Rome to get around to it. In addition to those who can testify personally to her holiness, her decades of direct service to the poor through the Catholic Worker movement and political activism have been chronicled in many a biography as well as in her own writings. Day died in 1980 at her beloved Maryhouse in New York City, surrounded by the poor whom she served for so many years in a life that, it seems, will one day be officially recognized as saintly.

From 2012 to 2017, I worked as an editor at Orbis Books, the Maryknoll-sponsored publishing house devoted to books on social justice, liberation theology, and emerging theological movements of the past half-century (and the publisher of this book!). The publisher and editor in chief, Robert Ellsberg, had been a close friend of Dorothy and the managing editor of the *Catholic Worker* newspaper in the late 1970s. Among his many literary efforts has been a decades-long project to bring all of Dorothy's writings to a larger public.

Most of us know of her famous memoir, *The Long Loneliness*; but less often read are her other books, diaries, and her many articles for the *Catholic Worker* and elsewhere throughout her life. Some of those articles were spicier than others; consider a 1933 essay, "The Diabolic Plot," in which she defended communism and explained why most Catholics misunderstand it. "It is when the Communists are good that they are dangerous. And the trouble with many Catholics is that they do not recognize this dangerous goodness," she wrote. Don't tell the Napa Institute!

Born in 1897 in New York City to a middle-class family, Dorothy Day was raised in Oakland, California, and Chicago. During the time she attended the University of Illinois, her interest in justice grew and she became a socialist. When her studies ended, she moved to New York, where she wrote for various socialist newspapers and worked as a nurse. She is variously described as a socialist, an anarchist, a bohemian, or all of the above during this time period. In November 1917 she was arrested at the White House, protesting in favor of women's suffrage, the first of many arrests.

In 1920, Day married Berkeley Tobey (how's that for a name?), with whom she spent a year in Europe before returning to New York City and filing for divorce. The sale of the movie rights to a semi-autobiographical novel about her life brought her enough money to buy a cottage on Staten Island, where she lived from 1925 to 1929. During that time, she met Forster Batterham, with whom she would have a daughter, Tamar, in 1926. While Batterham remained strongly opposed to organized religion, Dorothy found herself increasingly drawn to Catholicism, and had Tamar baptized in July 1927. And in December of that year, Day entered the Catholic Church.

A major turn in her life came in 1932, when Day met a quixotic fellow by the name of Peter Maurin, a fan of distributism and an advocate of "houses of hospitality" in America's crowded urban centers. Day joined with him in establishing St. Joseph's House of Hospitality in New York and in publishing the *Catholic Worker*, a pioneering paper (sold then and now for a penny) that promoted their movement, itself eventually called the "Catholic Worker." Similar communities sprang up in the years that followed in cities, suburbs, and even rural farming areas, all devoted to direct service to the poor and marginalized and all offering a prophetic alternative to American-style capitalism. As a pacifist and also a strong advocate for organized labor, Day got arrested for both causes countless times over the course of her life.

The Long Loneliness was published in 1952, and has since become a spiritual classic read by millions. Recent years have seen numerous biographies of Day and the Catholic Worker movement, as well as the publication of many of her diaries and letters edited by Robert Ellsberg. In 2023, a new edition of her book *From Union Square to Rome* was released with a foreword by Pope Francis, at the same time her case for canonization was under review.

In support of her canonization, Robert Ellsberg wrote in 2015, "If I take the opportunity now to explain my reasons, it is not to change the minds of those who believe Dorothy Day is unworthy to be called a saint," he wrote. "There are some, for instance, who believe that she was a heretic, a secret Communist or, in the words of the state senator from Virginia who felt compelled to warn the pope, a woman of 'loathsome character.' Those for whom I write are instead the many deep admirers and even followers of Dorothy Day who have no doubts about her holiness but are skeptical or suspicious of the process of canonization."

Why? Some of Dorothy's followers fear that by naming her a saint the church will turn her into "a pious cutout—shorn of her prophetic and radical edges—or use her to promote some agenda that was not her own. Others question the investment of resources that might better be used for the poor."

Part of Ellsberg's reasoning for supporting the cause—beyond his conviction that she was indeed a saint—came from his study of her own writings. "We are all called to be saints," she had once written, "and we might as well get over our bourgeois fear of the name. We might also get used to recognizing the fact that there is some of the saint in all of us."

She also recognized the complexity of the modern age, the reality that many people no longer sought holiness in their lives. They, "if they were asked, would say diffidently that they do not profess to be saints; indeed they do not want to be saints. And yet the saint is the holy man, the 'whole man,' the integrated man. We all wish to be that." That is some food for thought for anyone who thinks a life of Christian discipleship is a hindrance to becoming a fully integrated person.

Dorothy also spoke truth to power—which is certainly why powerful men have stooped to calling her loathsome—and her targets were sometimes the princes of the church. "In all history popes and bishops and father abbots seem to have been blind and power loving and greedy. I never expected leadership from them," she once wrote. "It is the saints that keep appearing all thru [*sic*] history who keep things going," a quote that didn't seem to make it into Cardinal Dolan's homily.

"The same woman who attended Mass every day of her adult life, refused to hear any criticism of the Pope, and accepted Vatican teachings on all matters concerning sex, birth control, and abortion," wrote Mike Mastromatteo in a 2020 review of the biography *Dorothy Day: Dissenting Voice of the American Century*, by John Loughery and Blythe Randolph, "could be blistering in her remarks about priests who lived in well-appointed rectories and turned a blind eye to racial segregation in their own parishes, bishops who were allies of the rich and powerful, and Catholic writers who viewed patriotism and faith as equivalent virtues, who were more concerned with the threat of 'godless Communism' than the needs of the poor."

Devotees of Dorothy Day may recall that official recognition of her saintly life came from the mayor of New York City before it came from the Vatican: on March 25, 2021, Bill de Blasio announced that a 4,500-passenger boat on the Staten Island Ferry line would be named for Dorothy Day. "How appropriate that a ferry transporting people would honor a believing apostle of peace, justice, and charity who devoted her life to moving people from war to peace, from emptiness to fullness, from isolation to belonging," commented Cardinal Dolan at the time.

When the boat was commissioned on November 4, 2022, Dorothy Day's granddaughter, Martha Hennessy, spoke at the ceremony. "In these days of global instability, let us use this moment to remember her efforts to make peace," Hennessy, herself a longtime social-justice activist, said.

It's fitting, isn't it?—the Staten Island Ferry is that most communist of plots: a free public amenity.

7

SIGRID UNDSET
Truth and Fiction

Who's your favorite Catholic novelist? I used to ask this question of friends and colleagues when I taught a course on the subject at Fordham University. Over time I found different answers came based on the generation and life station of those I asked. For example, priests of a certain age would answer surprisingly consistently, offering a name that, now, might surprise: Sigrid Undset.

The winner of the Nobel Prize in Literature in 1928, Undset was a leading figure of the Norwegian intelligentsia in the 1920s and 1930s. When she fled to the United States after the Nazi invasion of Norway in 1940, she became a frequent contributor to U.S. literary and political journals. More significantly for those who listed her as their fave, however, was her *Kristin Lavransdatter* trilogy of novels.

The Rev. Robert E. Lauder, a frequent film and book reviewer for many Catholic magazines over the years and himself a teacher of many classes on the Catholic novel, argued that *Kristin Lavransdatter* "is the greatest Catholic novel ever written." And Raymond Schroth, S.J., a longtime editor at both *Commonweal* and *America*, recalled his father reading *Kristin Lavransdatter* aloud to his mother as she

26

knitted in the evenings. After entering the Jesuits years later, Schroth discovered the trilogy "to be the favorite of Jesuit seminarians in the late 1950s, perhaps because for many, still in their teens, it was a rare romantic experience."

Born in 1882 in Kalundborg, Denmark, Sigrid Undset moved to Norway with her family when she was two and grew up in Oslo (known then as Kristiania), the capital of Norway. She published her first novel at the age of twenty-five; her gritty depictions of the life of women in the city (including tales of adultery) made her something of an avant-garde author in the years before the First World War. When she converted to Catholicism in 1924 it caused a stir in heavily Lutheran Norway—especially as the first volume of *Kristin Lavransdatter* was enjoying success at home and abroad. Soon after the third volume of that trilogy was published in 1927, she was awarded the Nobel Prize.

The chairman of the Nobel Committee noted that Undset was that *rara avis* among Nobel recipients: she received the award "while still in her prime, an homage rendered to a poetic genius whose roots must be in a great and well-ordered spirit."

Settling in Brooklyn Heights after fleeing the Nazis in Norway (where her son was killed in battle), Undset began speaking and writing against totalitarianism and both Hitler and Stalin. She also began publishing essays on literature.

In one 1942 essay on "Truth and Fiction," Undset began with a bit of wisdom that an "old Norwegian farmer's wife once handed out to me, as the principle on which she had been brought up and in her turn had brought up a large family of fine men and women: 'Never tell a lie. And don't tell a truth, unless it is necessary.'" (Those surprised at such a spicy beginning would not have read Undset's debut novel, whose first line was "I have been unfaithful to my husband.")

"To the Catholic writer," Undset continued, "the whole world of facts and truths behind the facts will appear in relation to the Ultimate Origin from which everything emanates." Returning to her opening adage, she reminded her audience never to tell a lie, and "tell the truths you have to. Even if they are grim, preposterous, shocking. After all, we Catholics ought to acknowledge what a shocking business human life is. Our race has been revolting against its Creator since the beginning of time. Revolt, betrayal, denial, or indifference, sloth, laziness—which of us has not been guilty in one or more or all of these sins some time or other?"

But also remember, she said: "You have to tell other and more cheering truths, too: of the Grace of God and the endeavor of strong and loyal, or weak but trusting souls, and also of the natural virtues of man created in the Image of God, an image it is very hard to efface entirely."

8

LEONARD FEENEY
To Hell with You All

The name Leonard Feeney has faded somewhat into history, but there was a time when he made headlines around the United States for his ideological battle with the Catholic Church and his eventual excommunication. Long before the pugnacious priest insisted that the notion that "there is no salvation outside the church" was a hard and fast rule and formed his own schismatic community, he was an accomplished poet and satirist. Then he broke bad.

Feeney worked at *America* from 1936 to 1942 as the literary editor (he remains to date the only *America* literary editor to be excommunicated—fingers crossed!), writing book reviews, short stories, poems, and the occasional broadside against popular culture. He had previously published *Fish on Friday*, a collection of humorous essays on theological topics that remains in print; Cardinal John O'Connor, the archbishop of New York from 1984 to 2000, said in 1994 that he read *Fish on Friday* every Lent. After a brief stint at Weston College outside Boston to serve as (wait for it) a "Professor of Sacred Eloquence," in 1943 Feeney was appointed the spiritual director of the St. Benedict Center, a Catholic student center adjacent to Harvard University in Cambridge, Massachusetts.

Feeney was immediately popular for his wit and his rousing sermons; even during his time in New York, he had preached often at St. Patrick's Cathedral as well as on the radio. Catholic students from Harvard and Radcliffe were showing up in droves for the first few years of Feeney's tenure, with some leaving school to become full-time devotees of the St. Benedict Center. By one estimate, the center prompted over two hundred converts to Catholicism and over one hundred vocations to religious life under Feeney.

Feeney's downfall began with his interpretation of *"extra ecclesiam nulla salus,"* the Catholic doctrine that there is no salvation outside the church. Catholics had long allowed for exceptions and for the presence of God's grace to bring salvation to nonbelievers—otherwise the vast majority of humans who have ever lived are in hell—but Feeney wouldn't have it. To interpret the teaching as anything but an absolute rule smacked to him of religious indifferentism and of a failure to uphold eternal teachings. Soon his sermons and talks on the subject took on an uglier and more pugnacious tone.

Two people who didn't care for Feeney's rhetoric were Robert F. Kennedy, who stormed out of one of Feeney's lectures, and Evelyn Waugh, who after hearing him speak called Feeney "a case of demonic possession."

In late 1948, Feeney's Jesuit provincial transferred him to the College of the Holy Cross in Worcester, Massachusetts. Feeney refused to go. When four teachers at Boston College and Boston College High School were fired for teaching Feeney's hardline approach to salvation, Feeney published a fiery defense of the four—and suggested both his Jesuit superiors and Cardinal Richard Cushing, archbishop of Boston, were advocating heresy. Cushing removed his faculties as a priest and forbade Catholics to visit the St. Benedict Center. Feeney was then dismissed by the Jesuits for disobedience. Finally, in 1953, Pope Pius XII excommunicated him.

Rome moves slowly. Already by 1951, Feeney was delivering weekly speeches on the Boston Common, railing against Cushing and the Jesuits but also taking vicious and bigoted swipes at perceived enemies right and left. The *Harvard Crimson* reported that Feeney had vowed to "rid our city of every coward liberal Catholic, Jew dog, Protestant brute, and 33rd degree Mason who is trying to suck the soul from good Catholics and sell the true faith for greenbacks." Awkward.

He and many of his devoted followers—then known as the Slaves of the Immaculate Heart of Mary—eventually moved to Still River, Massachusetts. While some members later formed a new schismatic community in New Hampshire, the Still River community is in full communion with the Catholic Church.

Reading Feeney's early book reviews, you quickly get a sense of the pugnacity that would become his trademark; he was sort of a Jesuit Michiko Kakutani, an intimidating reviewer with strong opinions and a willingness to deride even cultural icons like Robert Frost and Ernest Hemingway. One 1937 essay by Feeney was titled "Resentments and Raptures Concerning My Contemporaries," and its contents did not disappoint.

What did he think of the aforementioned Hemingway? "Do you know a good way to convince ladies who adore he-men that you are a he-man and not a sissy? Raise a challenging mustache," Feeney wrote. "Write a humorless book full of unabridged hells and damns and kindred phrases in the field of sex, and then come out blatantly in favor of the Loyalists' cause in Spain."

Do you remember the comedian Ed Wynn? He was so big in the 1930s that he turned down the role of the wizard in *The Wizard of Oz*, believing it too minor. For decades he also had a radio show. Feeney didn't care for it: "Ed Wynn: The only thing worse than him on the radio is all static."

But it was Robert Frost who really ground Feeney's gears. In a 1936 review, Feeney made his feelings clear. "It is hard to believe that he chops nearly as much wood as he pretends to, or that cows, hens, and barnyards are his chief loves. He has been known to enjoy the tea life of social England and is at present a professor of poetry in a college," he wrote. "There is evidence in *A Further Range* that Robert Frost is in danger of mistaking his own powers. His *Build Soil—A Political Pastoral* is exceptionally bad."

After Feeney's death in 1978, Avery Dulles, S.J., wrote a long eulogy for him, noting that Feeney had been reconciled to the church in 1974. "There are certain texts from the Bible that I can never read without hearing, in my imagination, the voice and intonations of Leonard Feeney," wrote Dulles, who had been among the founders of the St. Benedict Center. With Feeney's death, "the United States lost one of its most colorful, talented, and devoted priests. The obituary notices, on the whole, tended to overlook the brilliance of his career and to concentrate only on the storm of doctrinal controversy associated with his name in the late 1940s and early 1950s."

Dulles, who would later be named a cardinal of the church, called Feeney one of the most skilled orators he had ever met, saying, "he had an incomparable gift for putting the deepest mysteries in the simplest terms." While acknowledging that things had gone awry for Feeney, Dulles remained appreciative of him for his gifts but also for his determination. "In an age of accommodation and uncertainty, he went to extremes in order to avoid the very appearance of compromise," Dulles wrote. "With unstinting generosity he placed all his talents and energies in the service of the faith as he saw it."

9

MARY GORDON
"What Kind of Catholic Are You?"

"*Catholic* means only one of three things: a regrettable tendency to lean right, an appetite for sexual repression, an inborn or early-developed talent for blind obedience." Mary Gordon wrote this in 2021, not to reflect her own sense of what it means to be Catholic—but in fact to express the way so many people view the church in an age of sex abuse scandals, Trumpers, and the diminishment of mainstream Christian denominations. She was working on a book project at the time titled *What Kind of Catholic Are You?*

Gordon, who over the years has published dozens of novels, memoirs, and short story collections, has always had a complicated—well, let's say nuanced—relationship with Catholicism, and so it rankles her when people ask her, "Why are you still Catholic?"

"The answer that usually shuts people up," she writes, "is that 'the terms are large.'"

For her new project, Gordon came up with pairs of people who credit their Catholicism for their ideas—except that some of their ideas are diametrically opposed to each other. Bill O'Reilly is linked with Stephen Colbert; Anna Quindlen forms an odd couple with Ross Douthat; Rachel Maddow meets Laura Ingraham; and so on. "I have many more affini-

34

ties with some of these people than others, just as I have more affinities with some of the fictional characters I have created than with others. But I am not creating characters; these are real people with real lives not under my control," Gordon writes. "But I hope that some of my novelist's habits of mind and language can be of use as I try to enter into an understanding of lives in some ways similar to, and in others very different from, my own."

In other words, Gordon has no interest in playing "an extended game of *gotcha*" to prove who is and who isn't *really* Catholic: "I believe that because the people about whom I am writing share with me a vocabulary, a set of images, and shared practices (after all, when we hear the 'Hail Mary,' we all know the words), there are some firm grounds on which we can all stand."

I first encountered Mary Gordon's writing when I read *Final Payments*, the brilliant and emotionally searing 1978 novel that tells the story of Isabel Moore, a young Irish Catholic woman finding her way in life after the death of a domineering and complicated father for whom she had cared for years. I have used the book in courses I taught on Catholic novels several times since, because it encompasses so many of the themes I wanted to explore with my students: the reality of change in a church that so often sees itself as immutable, the perdurance of a sacramental imagination in an American context that so often rejects it, the difficulty of seeking holiness and personal integrity in a setting where the two goals can seem to conflict. To my mind, Isabel Moore was a powerful characterization of the life and times of so many U.S. Catholics then and now.

Gordon remains a prolific novelist, with 2020 marking the publication of *Payback*, her ninth. In his review of the book,

Mike Mastromatteo notes that "readers familiar with Gordon's earlier fiction will almost certainly warm to *Payback*," a novel that "offers complex characters who inevitably force readers to consider ideas well beyond the mundane."

The novel centers on a Rhode Island art teacher, Agnes Vaughan, and her lifetime of remorse for failing a vulnerable student decades before. The student, meanwhile, has spent forty years orchestrating payback for what she perceives as her teacher's cruelty. Eventually the student becomes the host of a reality television show that allows victims of wrongdoing to confront their tormentors—"a kind of trash television," Mastromatteo writes, "where the 'owed' win a humiliating form of justice."

What results is "a compelling consideration of the cult of victimization and its impact on social concepts of justice, forgiveness, and healing." "Reality TV: there was nothing real about it," Gordon writes in *Payback*. "It was an invention, a shape-making, as fictional as any fiction, more so because it denied its fictiveness, made a fiction of truth and a truth of fiction."

Getting back to *Final Payments* (I'm still a little obsessed). In her 1978 review, Mary Sabolik praised Gordon's story for capturing the experience of young women of a certain era. "Aside from the specifics of class and locale, there are, for any young woman brought up in the Catholic Church, many jolts of recognition in this book, as Isabel's natural impulses clash with her religious sensibilities," Sabolik wrote. "As the novel's central figure, Isabel is a richly complicated woman, at once vulnerable and defiant." Gordon, Sabolik wrote, captured the petty cruelties as well as the noble impulses of everyday life: "While the author's treatment of character is perceptive and sympathetic, it is also unflinchingly honest."

Gordon later published *The Shadow Man: A Daughter's Search for Her Father*, a memoir of her research into the life of the man who had died in 1957 when she was seven, and with whom the father in *Final Payments* shared many characteristics. Gordon found that much of what she knew about her father was the result of family myths and his own deceptive narrative about himself. His name, birthplace, background, and catalog of published writings, she discovered in her search, were all mostly fiction. It creates a curious *frisson* for a novelist, does it not, when you realize that someone you tried to render in fiction had done the same with his supposed facts? What did Gordon say above about making "a fiction of truth and a truth of fiction"?

A decade later, Gordon wrote another memoir, this time about her relationship with her mother. "Unflinchingly honest" also describes Gordon's prose in *Circling My Mother*, where she writes dispassionately about a complicated and difficult woman who faced physical obstacles and eventually dementia with a preternatural stubbornness. "She has become my words," Gordon writes near the close of the book, "or dust. Both. How is it possible to comprehend this?"

You can imagine my delight (followed by surprise) when, in 2022, Mary Gordon wrote to me at *America* and asked if she could review a book for the magazine. "Yes," I prevaricated, "absolutely one hundred percent yes." Yet her selection was a curious one: Kellyanne Conway's memoir, *Here's the Deal*. Why on earth would Mary Gordon want to review a book by Donald J. Trump's former counselor?

"People who know me even slightly are shocked when they hear me say that I have a lot in common with Kellyanne Conway," Gordon wrote in her review. "How can I, a left-wing feminist who went into four years of mourning at

Donald Trump's election, feel any kinship with the woman who arguably made his election possible? How can I, a person who prides myself on being devoted to precision of language, have any connection with the author of the phrase 'alternate facts'? But my early life is eerily similar to hers."

She's not wrong. Both were raised by single mothers; both attended Catholic schools through high school; both have had careers that exceeded the expectations of their peers, in part because both are "unafraid of standing up to powerful men." That might be where it ends—Gordon notes that Conway was "New Jersey Blueberry Princess" as a young woman, and her family's fortune was largely derived from the underworld activities of a gangster named "Jimmy the Brute"—but the similarities are striking.

What one does with that upbringing becomes a crucial question for Gordon, however: Does one value the gifts of a Catholic childhood while striving to winnow the wheat from the chaff? Does one choose tolerance over suspicion, compassion over cruelty? The answer to those questions might answer for Gordon her earlier question: what kind of Catholic are you?

10

CHRISTOPHER LASCH
The Marxist Traditionalists Love

W hat does a reader make of a secular Marxist who is beloved by traditionalist Catholics? Of an author who was a favorite both of Jimmy Carter and of Steve Bannon? Of a thinker heavily influenced by Sigmund Freud who made himself *persona non grata* among many mental health professionals for his jeremiads against contemporary psychology? You don't hear about him as much anymore—he died in 1994—but there was a time when Christopher "Kit" Lasch was all but a household name.

Lasch became famous with his 1979 book, *The Culture of Narcissism: American Life in an Age of Diminishing Expectations*, though he was probably at his polemical and incisive best in the posthumous 1995 essay collection, *The Revolt of the Elites and the Betrayal of Democracy*. There's something in both for everyone to hate, and yet take a look at the footnotes in some of your favorite books: Lasch appears in the works of everyone from the philosopher Charles Taylor to the political scientist Patrick Deneen to the late Jesuit environmentalist and theologian David Toolan, S.J.

Regularly writing for *Commonweal*, Lasch was also a contributing editor to the *New Oxford Review*, two journals that could not possibly be further apart on the Catholic spectrum, and his name came up often enough in Catholic media for various reasons. When San Francisco Archbishop John R. Quinn wrote a critique in 1991 of a proposal to distribute condoms to schoolchildren, he approvingly cited Lasch's commentary in *The Culture of Narcissism* on government attempts "to erode and appropriate the authority and the role of parents in regard to their children."

Eleven years later, Philadelphia Archbishop Charles J. Chaput, a prelate not often associated with Archbishop Quinn's ecclesial views, also cited Lasch in an essay on Cardinal Walter Kasper's ecclesiology for Lasch's description of modern Americans as "locked in a permanent present, permanently restless, permanently eager for change," often at the expense of tradition and stability, in churches just as much as anywhere else.

In 2015, I had occasion to return to Lasch myself in a book review I was writing of Elizabeth Lunbeck's *The Americanization of Narcissism*. No fan of Lasch, Lunbeck described her book as a "mission to rescue the concept of narcissism" and to return it to the realm of psychoanalysis rather than cultural critique. She argued that much of what Lasch saw as narcissistic behavior in American life was actually a welcome increase in levels of self-esteem and assertiveness, and that some degree of narcissism is helpful in the development of ambition, creativity, and empathy. (In her defense, the book was published before the election of Donald Trump.)

Born in Omaha, Nebraska, in 1932, Lasch was the son of a philosophy professor mother and a Rhodes Scholar father who later won the Pulitzer Prize for editorials criticizing the Vietnam War. Lasch himself attended Harvard University, where his roommate was—no joke—John Updike. "He writes poetry, stories, and draws cartoons and sends all of these to various magazines. He has even had a few things accepted," Lasch told his parents about Updike. "He is more industrious than I, but I think his stuff lacks perception and doesn't go very deep. He is primarily a humorist. As he himself admits, he is probably a hack." Updike later wrote a story about their time together, "The Christian Roommates," which was later turned into a TV movie in 1984.

After receiving his doctorate in history from Columbia University, Lasch taught for a time at the University of Iowa and Northwestern University before moving to the University of Rochester, where he taught from 1970 to 1994. Between 1962 and 1977 he published five books that inveighed against American-style capitalism but also offered pointed critiques of progressive politics, including his 1969 *The Agony of the American Left,* a political position that earned him labels ranging from cultural conservative to neo-Marxist gadfly.

When *The Culture of Narcissism* was published in 1979, its condemnation of the therapeutic mindset he believed was overtaking American community life firmly established Lasch as an important cultural critic and public intellectual. Soon after *The Culture of Narcissism* made the bestseller lists, then-President Jimmy Carter invited Lasch to the White House, and some of the book's themes found their way into Carter's infamous "malaise" speech in 1979. One can imagine this line from Carter's nationally televised address coming straight from Lasch's pen:

> In a nation that was proud of hard work, strong families, close-knit communities, and our faith in God, too many of us now tend to worship self-indulgence

and consumption. Human identity is no longer defined by what one does, but by what one owns.

Because Lasch was critical of divorce and legal abortion and was a strong proponent of the nuclear family, he was often associated in the 1980s with Reaganite politics, though he despised and often wrote against the libertarian thread running through 1980s American conservatism and was no fan of Reagan (even less so of William F. Buckley). His later writings had a strong focus on the negative effects of the American obsession with progress, including *The True and Only Heaven: Progress and Its Critics* (1991).

I first encountered Lasch as a college student in a course on political philosophy where we read several of the essays that would later appear in *The Revolt of the Elites*. In those essays, Lasch excoriated globalization and the increasing economic gap between the top 20 percent of American earners and the rest, arguing that the cosmopolitan cadres that increasingly dominated political and cultural life had little interest in accepting the obligations of citizenship or the duty to support their fellow citizens. Such "world citizens," he wrote, had no reason to support traditional family structures, working-class citizens, or the increasing number of Americans afflicted with crime, poverty, addiction, or mental illness.

The Revolt of the Elites made Lasch something of a populist icon, which explains some of his appeal to the likes of Steve Bannon despite Lasch's lifelong criticism of capitalism and the free market. But it also included some of his most religious thought, including "The Soul of Man under Secularism," an essay that trenchantly observed that our belief in "the right to be happy"—that uniquely American addition to Locke's universal rights—was itself psychologically immature. The truly effective counter in American life was religious belief and practice, Lasch noted: a recognition of the transcendence of God and the acceptance of limitations on our ambitions and appetites as a result.

As he often did, Lasch comes across as quite the grump on the subject—but as usual, he had a point.

11

Toni Morrison
A Theology of the Passion

During a recent Banned Books Week, library employees around the country brought attention to current and historical attempts at censorship and silencing of authors. Joined by many colleagues in publishing and education, they sought to spotlight specific authors and subjects targeted by school districts and public libraries around the country and by individuals and groups seeking to have books removed from shelves that to them might be "offensive" or "indoctrinating." One author's name came up numerous times: she has had not one, not two, but three of her books on the "most banned" lists: Toni Morrison.

Both *Beloved* and *The Bluest Eye* have been targeted repeatedly in recent years for removal from libraries and schools. The former won the Pulitzer Prize for Fiction in 1988. Another of Morrison's novels, *Song of Solomon*, won the National Book Critics Circle Award in 1977, but has also been the target of challenges by school boards in three different states.

According to the American Library Association, the most common grounds for challenging books on school reading lists are the depiction of LGBTQ lifestyles, sexual material, contentious religious viewpoints, profanity, and content that addresses racism and police brutality. In the case of Morrison, the criticism aimed at her books tends to be more vague—because the real issue seems to be that Morrison's fiction makes white people uncomfortable.

It should.

Beloved is a difficult book to read, not because the book is lurid or exploitative or crass, but because it is relentless in its depiction of the horrors white people inflicted on Black people both during and after slavery. The casual and unreflective violence of our culture comes through in almost every interaction. Morrison doesn't water down her stories. Rape, incest, pedophilia, and physical violence are present in her books because they were and are present in the real lives of people very much like Morrison's characters. As the character Baby Suggs notes in *Beloved*, "Not a house in the country ain't packed to its rafters with some dead Negro's grief."

Examining the role of the Catholic faith in American fiction since the Second Vatican Council, Nick Ripatrazone writes about Morrison in his book *Longing for an Absent God*. He posits that Morrison (who became a Catholic in her teens with "Toni" a shortening of her confirmation name, Anthony) makes strong connections between Black suffering and Christ's own, especially in the novels *Beloved* and *The Bluest Eye*. "Morrison's theology is one of the Passion: of scarred bodies, public execution, and private penance," he writes.

Morrison's characters are resilient and strong, but inevitably in situations where the alternative is death, either of the body or of the soul. Her characters also often thrive in a liminal space between the natural and the supernatural. "A belief in a world other than one in which blacks are dehumanized and devalued helps her characters thrive, as it did for Morrison's very own family members," wrote Nadra Nittle in a 2017 appreciation of Morrison:

> She remarked during a 1983 interview that her characters are high-functioning—they are able to navigate day-to-day life in a racially stratified society while also having run-ins with the supernatural. Steeped in the African-American spiritual tradition, her characters are at ease when they encounter otherworldly or extraordinary forces. This is especially true of *Beloved* and *Song of Solomon*.

In 2021, Nittle published *Toni Morrison's Spiritual Vision*, in which she examined the ways in which faith, spirituality, a storytelling culture, and Morrison's own feminism intersected and complemented each other in her books. Nittle also noted that despite the often-cruel worlds Morrison's books explore, they all share another common theme: "Healing—through religious syncretism, racial pride, and the wisdom of elders—is the crux of Morrison's fiction," she wrote.

"Toni Morrison's characters always find faith in themselves, in God, and in the circumstances of life, without always explicitly naming it as faith," wrote Boreta Singleton in a review of *Toni Morrison's Spiritual Vision*. "As Nittle notes, these discoveries lead them to new realizations and moments of deep awareness about life and love. The reader can see God in all areas of Morrison's characters' circumstances—in the 'magic,' in the pain and suffering, and in the call to healing and wholeness that leads to life."

While Morrison was honored with the Nobel Prize in Literature in 1993, it was in 2012 that President Barack Obama gave her the Presidential Medal of Freedom for her body of work and her advocacy of justice. On August 5, 2019,

Morrison died at the age of eighty-eight. A memorial service several months later in New York City included eulogies by Angela Davis, Oprah Winfrey, Fran Lebowitz, Ta-Nehisi Coates, and Michael Ondaatje.

In a 2019 tribute to Morrison after her death, Tia Noelle Pratt noted how important it was for Black readers to have a writer like Morrison, who did not center her stories from a white perspective or adopt a "white gaze" in her narration. Rather, she sought to give a hearing to the genuine experiences of people who were too often voiceless: "Toni Morrison's work conveyed the pain, sacrifice, and trauma that exemplifies so much of the African-American experience."

12

Cormac McCarthy
"All the Subtle Demonisms of Life and Thought"

One of the more unsettling characters in American fiction over the past half-century is surely Judge Holden, the huge, pale, hairless sadist who serves as the antagonist of Cormac McCarthy's 1985 novel *Blood Meridian*. A friend of mine insists that Judge Holden was McCarthy's Moby-Dick, a symbol of ultimate evil and "all the subtle demonisms of life and thought," to quote *Moby-Dick*, that haunted humanity's dreams. My friend could plot out Judge Holden's whole character arc, he claimed, as a parallel to the huge, pale, hairless whale that bedeviled Melville's Captain Ahab—and indeed, McCarthy once listed *Moby-Dick* as his favorite work of fiction. (He also wrote a screenplay called "Whales and Men," which has nothing to do with *Moby-Dick*.) But does *Blood Meridian* hold up to *Moby-Dick*?

More than a few famous writers have claimed just that about McCarthy's work, including David Foster Wallace and Harold Bloom, the latter calling McCarthy "the worthy disciple both of Melville and of Faulkner." The author of twelve novels, McCarthy won the National Book Award for *All the*

Pretty Horses and the Pulitzer Prize for *The Road*. When Toni Morrison died in 2019, some critics called McCarthy the nation's best chance for another Nobel Prize in Literature. After a sixteen-year hiatus, he published two novels in 2022, *The Passenger* and *Stella Maris*.

But after McCarthy died at the age of eighty-nine on June 13, 2022, many obituaries noted that McCarthy's writing also had a dark, disturbing timbre not usually found among those proposed as great American novelists. "McCarthy has always nursed a perverse streak," wrote Robert Rubsam in his March 2023 review of *The Passenger* and *Stella Maris*—something more than a few readers of McCarthy's early novels likely consider a serious understatement. In addition to the relentless violence depicted in many of his books, McCarthy had little use for stories of redemption or of the possibility of good triumphing over evil in a fallen world. Instead he invariably told the tale of instinct-driven men (almost always men) whose base natures went unchecked by society or morality. Alongside the exploration of base nature, religious imagery abounds in all his books.

"Much like Flannery O'Connor, McCarthy was surrounded by evangelical caricatures of his family's faith, and that dissonance is reflected in his pulpy and visceral fictional iconography," wrote Nick Ripatrazone in a 2014 review of Bryan Giemza's *Sorrow's Rigging*, a study of McCarthy, Don DeLillo, and Robert Stone. Giemza, Ripatrazone wrote, "reaches a smart conclusion: McCarthy's Catholicism is revealed in 'literally liturgical' prose, in a 'fascination with the mystery of evil,' all delivered in a 'heretical interrogation' of the religion." That McCarthy is "less sacramental than eschatological does not negate his Catholic background."

McCarthy was raised Catholic, with his brother William

McCarthy spending a decade as a Jesuit before leaving in 1968 before ordination to the priesthood. Former *America* literary editor Patrick Samway, S.J., once noted after speaking with McCarthy that he "knew things only a Jesuit would know." (Why is that comment so terrifying?) However, McCarthy himself drifted from the church after high school, and his (rare) interviews over the years shed little light on what faith, if any, he professed.

The violence and depravity that marked the novels of McCarthy's middle career, including his "border trilogy" and *Blood Meridian*, became more muted in McCarthy's later novels, and his 2006 novel, *The Road*, is a stark departure from his earlier work. Amid the carnage and cannibalism (and yes, there's still plenty of both) committed by those trying to survive in a dying world, his two unnamed protagonists in that novel share a loving father–son relationship that feels remarkably authentic for a writer not known for explorations of human love.

In a 2007 review of *The Road*, John B. Breslin, S.J., linked McCarthy's tale to a long literary history of apocalyptic novels born out of the fear of a global nuclear war. He noted that "Cormac McCarthy has crafted a lean fable in this book that spells out the horrors we may face in our atomic future, but he also gives us hope for our continuance with the story of a father who gives all to his son, and stranger who takes the father's place when all seems lost."

Many of McCarthy's novels were made into movies, and some obituaries mentioned that McCarthy had been working on a screenplay for a film adaptation of *Blood Meridian*, to be directed by John Hillcoat, who helmed the film adaptation of *The Road*.

Who would play Judge Holden? I wonder. And how could the events of such a novel be distilled into a two-hour movie? And let's be honest—would the Motion Picture Association of America have to create a new rating category, one far, far beyond NC-17?

13

Brian Doyle
Tiny Miracles

One day at work recently, my colleague Kevin Clarke shared a poem from *Eureka Street,* an online journal published by the Australian Jesuits. The poem, "If we ever got to be what we so want to be," was a powerful reflection on finding the beautiful and the divine amid life's struggles. It was also by Brian Doyle, a literary voice I cherished, and one that was lost too soon: Doyle died in 2017 at the age of sixty.

Like many of his readers, I was first exposed to Brian Doyle's writings through *Portland Magazine* and *Notre Dame Magazine,* two university journals he frequently published work in. And Doyle remained for many years the editor—no, the Svengali, but in a good way—of *Portland Magazine,* where he attracted prominent contributing artists and authors and consistently won awards for the magazine's content and design, including the Sibley Award in 2005 as the top university magazine in the country.

Doyle also wrote countless essays and poems for other journals over the years. Sometimes the poems felt more like prose, a style he called "proems"; sometimes the titles themselves were the length of a poem, as in his 2007 submission,

"On Cleaning Out a Friend's Refrigerator after His Exile to the Old Priests' Home."

Years ago, as an editor at Orbis Books, I had the chance to work with Doyle on a book of such proems, *How the Light Gets In*. (Yes, he wanted the Leonard Cohen reference: "There is a crack, a crack in everything / that's how the light gets in.") I've long lost our correspondence, which is a shame, because his emails were their own literary genre.

But it was in his prose essays that Doyle's literary gifts shone through most clearly. Proust may have had his madeleine, but Brian Doyle's capacious memory could be jolted by the sights and smells of a Catholic school gym. Essays on faith and fatherhood were intermixed over the years with reflections on everything from scapulars to the beauty of the smallest gestures at the Easter Vigil. He could be unconventional in topic and style, but he didn't often miss the mark in capturing a perfect tone of wonder.

"It was a delight to edit Doyle's prose," wrote his sometime editor Kerry Weber upon Doyle's death in 2017. "His unique style and tone created texts so tight that his manuscripts often were left relatively untouched by our editors, save some added punctuation intended to break up his paragraphs, which were filled with grace and unconcerned with grammar." ("I get teased a lot for my style," Doyle admitted in 2015. "People are saying, wow, a sentence will start on Tuesday and it doesn't end 'till Friday. But I want to write like people talk. I want to write like I'm speaking to you.")

Doyle also authored more than two dozen books, including short story anthologies, essay collections, poetry, and novels, including *Mink River*, *The Plover*, and *Martin Marten*. He was awarded the Pushcart Prize (for literary achievement in a small press) three times, and also received the American Academy of Arts and Letters Award.

Born in 1956 in New York City into a family of storytellers (his father, a journalist, was at one point the executive director of the Catholic Press Association), Doyle attended the University of Notre Dame. Then for many years he lived in Portland, Oregon, the setting for much of his fiction and nonfiction alike.

In November 2016, Doyle discovered he had what he called a "big honkin' brain tumor" and underwent surgery shortly after. He noted at the time that his diagnosis was terminal, and the surgery and ensuing chemotherapy were meant only to give him a year or two more. He died six months later in May, leaving behind a wife and three adult children.

In a tribute to Doyle, James M. Chesbro quoted the astonishing final line of Doyle's essay "Joyas Voladoras," a sentence so evocative the reader forgets that it runs on for the length of a paragraph:

> You can brick up your heart as stout and tight and hard and cold and impregnable as you possibly can and down it comes in an instant, felled by a woman's second glance, a child's apple breath, the shatter of glass in the road, the words *I have something to tell you*, a cat with a broken spine dragging itself into the forest to die, the brush of your mother's papery ancient hand in the thicket of your hair, the memory of your father's voice early in the morning echoing from the kitchen where he is making pancakes for his children.

"Doyle found ways to write about humanity with punch and vibrant courage and sentences that sometimes lasted for days, but his artistry granted us, his readers, access to the human condition we would not have had without his narrative prayers," Chesbro wrote. "He left them for us to read."

In a 2023 tribute to Doyle, Lindsay Schlegel noted that Doyle's most powerful work often reflected his fascination with the lives (and viewpoints) of children. "Doyle's fatherly love and joy shine throughout his work in every form," Schlegel wrote. "Here is a man who understood the beauty, the irreplaceability, the gift of even the shortest life, and who stood in awe and humility before this grace without ceasing."

Doyle's writing, she noted, "has the potential to stir this generation and the next to put down their smartphones (unless they're using them to read Doyle) and gape at every life with childlike wonder, to pause and see the more magnificent thing, the more tremendous gift toward which each tiny miracle points."

Perhaps Doyle at his best can be found in an essay from all the way back in 1994, "Naming," about his toddler daughter's exploration for the names of things—and his own thoughts on names in general. He closed the essay with a quintessential Brian Doyle coda, where it feels like the words are dancing:

> Some months ago Lily and I began to talk about God, whom she calls Gott. Usually she refers to him by name, but one night, when I asked her who takes care of Lily and Momma and Daddy, she thought for a moment and then smiled as sweetly and broadly as a dawn and I suddenly realized that her smile is the true name of God, which is a word that may be said silently and which names more things than we will ever know.

14

JAMES DICKEY
"Bare-Chested Bard"

Elsewhere in this book you can read of Moira Walsh, the fierce film critic who reviewed for numerous Catholic magazines and newspapers from 1947 to 1974, leaving many a movie vanquished on the page. Walsh had strong opinions about the moral purpose of good cinema and was not shy about criticizing the appearance of vice on screen. She also reviewed films for many years for the Legion of Decency, a Catholic group dedicated to identifying objectionable content in movies.

When I came across her 1972 review of *Deliverance*, then, I expected a fusillade of criticism launched at the dark, violent film, written by James Dickey and based on his 1970 novel of the same name and directed by John Boorman. "I expected to hate *Deliverance*," Walsh began, noting that "graphic extremes of violence" had ruined many another film, including Stanley Kubrick's *Clockwork Orange* (!!!). But wait:

> The line between purity of intent on one hand and sensationalism and exploitation on the other never seems that clear to me. Yet I have to eat my words

and tentatively accept the distinction because I found *Deliverance* a brilliant film.

What's this? "All sorts of theses swirl around in the material," she wrote. "Man against the elements, technology vs. nature, primitive vs. civilized man—but they belong there and are not forced on us in an arty or pretentious way."

Not a bad description of James Dickey's entire *oeuvre*, that.

The poet and novelist earned no shortage of honors and accolades throughout his career—his poetry collection *Buckdancer's Choice* won the National Book Award in 1966, when he was also the United States Poet Laureate. *Deliverance* (in which he also played a small role) made him a household name, and he read a poem at Jimmy Carter's 1977 presidential inauguration, but unlike other poets of his ilk, he always presented himself as the antithesis of pretension or even politesse. Of his appearance at Carter's inauguration, he told reporters: "Where else in history can you find it—the President and the poet, two Jimbos from Georgia."

Born in 1923 in Atlanta, Georgia, Dickey served in both World War II and Korea as a radar operator on P-61 fighter-bombers, an experience reflected in many of his later poems, including his famous "The Firebombing." After numerous teaching stints (and a memorable six-year run as a Manhattan advertising executive), Dickey settled in as writer in residence at the University of South Carolina in 1968. He published his first book, *Into the Stone and Other Poems*, in 1960, and followed it with more than twenty-five other volumes of poetry, essays, and journal collections.

His public persona of fighter pilot, champion athlete, and hard-drinking woodsman who wrote of "country surrealism" gave Dickey a tough-guy appeal, even as he was serving as a poetry consultant to the Library of Congress and corresponding with the brightest lights in the literary sky, from Ezra Pound to Robert Lowell to Denise Levertov.

Even Dickey's darker side ("I know what the monsters know," he once wrote in his journal), including a habit of exaggerating his own exploits, seemed to separate him from the tweed-and-elbow-patches professorial stereotypes, to say nothing of the standard image of a poet. And he enjoyed a good literary rumble: the literary critic and poet Dana Gioia once recounted a less-than-edifying encounter in which an angry Dickey confronted Gioia about his negative review of Dickey's poetry collection *Puella*, leading Goia to conclude, "It is often better not to meet the writers you admire."

Dickey's poems, wrote critic Paul Zweig in a 1990 essay for the *New York Times Book Review,* are "like richly modulated hollers; a sort of rough, American-style *bel canto* advertising its freedom from the constraints of ordinary language. Dickey's style is so personal, his rhythms so willfully eccentric, that the poems seem to swell up and overflow like that oldest of American art forms, the boast."

In a 1972 review of Dickey's *Sorties*, a collection of journal entries and essays, David R. Bishop criticized Dickey's journals for presenting "a ragged-edged silhouette of the author" but gushed of the essays that "Dickey writes with depth and fire, leading his reader to a world beyond sense, glimpsing the ecstasy of being human."

In a 1995 review of Dickey's *To the White Sea*, George J. Searles noted that "Dickey is powerfully adept at building suspense" and created a protagonist whose "resourcefulness in the face of unsurmountable odds elicits a grudging desire to learn his eventual fate, despite our revulsion at his grisly proclivities." While Searles was critical of Dickey's "tough guy" persona, he praised the book's "shimmering lyricism when the narrator rhapsodizes about the elemental beauty of nature. At those moments, Dickey the poet is much in evidence as the wording becomes quite evocative."

James Dickey died in 1997 in South Carolina of complications from lung disease after several years of declining health. His writerly genes were passed on: his son Christopher, who died in 2020, was a renowned foreign correspondent and memoirist, and James Dickey's daughter Bronwen (a longtime friend with whom I attended graduate school) is a contributing editor at the *Oxford American* and the author of *Pit Bull: The Battle over an American Icon.*

The *New York Times* suggested in Dickey's obituary that while *Deliverance* had brought the "bare-chested bard" the most fame, his poems about just about anything—from the Apollo 7 launch to football coaches (*Esquire* published his poem "For the Death of Vince Lombardi" in 1971) to backwoods archery—were his most remarkable achievements. Even the odes to athletes and hillbillies and fighter pilots were also "deceptively simple metaphysical poems that search the lakes and trees and workday fragments of his experience for a clue to the meaning of existence."

15

ALICE McDERMOTT
A Sacramental World

In 2009, Robert Lauder made the following claim about the "Catholic novel" in its better-known forms:

> At the risk of oversimplifying, the God who appears in the novels of [Graham] Greene, [Evelyn] Waugh, [François] Mauriac and [Flannery] O'Connor is the Transcendent Other, entering, sometimes suddenly, into the lives of the characters in the story. In those novels Francis Thompson's image of God as "The Hound of Heaven" is powerfully portrayed. The image is of God pursuing the sinner, and when an encounter between the novel's protagonist and God takes place, it is depicted very dramatically, even miraculously.

Recent decades, however, had brought a new kind of Catholic novelist to the fore: ones who were not writing out of the "church-against-culture" idiom of American Catholicism before the Second Vatican Council, nor necessarily depicting God as a "transcendent other." Chief among them, Lauder wrote, was Alice McDermott. "In

McDermott's world God could never be described as an outsider or an intruder," he wrote. "If poet Francis Thompson's 'The Hound of Heaven' illuminates Greene's work then poet Gerard Manley Hopkins' insight 'The world is charged with the grandeur of God' illuminates McDermott's. She sees creation as sacramental, and within this sacramental world grace works ever so subtly."

A native of Brooklyn, McDermott (now the Richard A. Macksey Professor of the Humanities at Johns Hopkins University) came of age in a rapidly changing nation and church, a theme reflected in many of her books. Her short stories have appeared everywhere from the *New Yorker* to *Seventeen* to *Commonweal*. In 2023, McDermott published *Absolution*, her ninth novel in a writing career that began with *A Bigamist's Daughter* in 1982. Her 1998 novel, *Charming Billy*, won the National Book Award, and three other novels—*That Night* (1987), *At Weddings and Wakes* (1992), and *After This* (2006)—were finalists for the Pulitzer Prize. She is also the author of a 2021 essay collection, *What about the Baby? Some Thoughts on the Art of Fiction*.

In a 2017 review of McDermott's novel *The Ninth Hour*, Jenny Shank wrote that "Alice McDermott has once again delivered a novel to ponder and cherish, from its moral quandaries down to its wry humor and hypnotic prose." Shank called her "perhaps today's pre-eminent American Catholic novelist, with three novels named as finalists for the Pulitzer Prize and one awarded the National Book Award (*Charming Billy*)." Many of McDermott's novels and stories are drawn from the Brooklyn Irish Catholic community that she grew up in, Shank noted, "but in none is it so thoroughly embedded as *The Ninth Hour*." Indeed, Irish Americans will recognize their families in many of McDermott's stories.

The Ninth Hour centers around a young woman and three nuns who serve as her adoptive aunts, and whose personalities and faith stories intersect, clash, and coexist in a Brooklyn convent. In a 2017 essay, Kevin Spinale, S.J., wrote of how much they reminded him of the formative influences on his own faith. "Catholicism—the history and culture of its American form—has been dyed into me like a garment taking on a color; I have absorbed Catholicism like a bolt of linen cloth taking on indigo," he wrote. "Catholicism cannot be washed out of me. And the principal dyers, the people who helped define me by my Catholic faith, were my aunts."

Some of these aunts were nuns, Spinale wrote, and all "rendered me Catholic through force of personality," women of "defiance, humor, fierce intelligence, and warmth." So too are the women of McDermott's novel, one in which men and church authorities "remain a ghostly presence" far from the action.

Robert Lauder once made an important point about McDermott's worldview. Her nuns are not like the protagonists of Graham Greene, lost or dissolute souls whom God finds in their moment of need; rather, the women of *The Ninth Hour* have spent all their lives in conversation with God—and they feel free to talk back a bit. While they live in a pre-Vatican II world, they speak less as cloistered nuns than as contemplatives in action, seeking to imitate Christ in their daily labors for the suffering poor of Brooklyn.

"In McDermott's novels God is the horizon toward which the characters are oriented, the atmosphere that surrounds them, the love in which they exist and move and have their being," Lauder wrote. Reading that, I immediately thought of *Charming Billy*—a novel whose characters do not experience dramatic changes in fortune, but simply persevere in a world full of lights and shadows.

"McDermott's novels are not so much about place as they are about people," wrote Angela Alaimo O'Donnell in a 2013 review of McDermott's novel *Someone*. "Her focus is on the ways in which human beings make a home in whatever world they happen to find themselves. And the key to that home is not location, location, location—it is love. This is McDermott's true subject, and she writes about it expertly, realistically, and poignantly."

While McDermott's previous work has largely centered on families in Brooklyn and Long Island, 2023's *Absolution* moves the bulk of the action to the other side of the world: Saigon during the Vietnam War. However, other themes—like Catholics struggling to live out their faith in the modern world, and the ins and outs of marital love—will be familiar to fans of McDermott's work.

I have been a fan of McDermott since I first read *Charming Billy* more than two decades ago, and have had occasion to return to that book several times since in teaching courses on Catholic fiction. I also know more than a few Irish American Catholics who say that reading that haunting but beautiful novel is like stepping back into their family history (and sometimes into parts of that history they didn't necessarily want to remember). Indeed, in a 1998 review of the novel, Gerard Reedy, S.J., noted that the "ethnic geography of Irish America, including the New York area, dominates *Charming Billy*."

I felt the same about *After This*, and not just because it's about a large Irish Catholic family named Keane!!!

16

PIERRE TEILHARD DE CHARDIN
An Evolving Universe of Grace

"To celebrate Mass in this land brought to my mind the prayer that the Jesuit Father Pierre Teilhard de Chardin offered to God exactly a hundred years ago, in the desert of Ordos, not far from here," said Pope Francis at the conclusion of Mass in Ulaanbaatar on Sunday, September 3, 2023, during his historic visit to Mongolia. Calling him "often misunderstood," the pope concluded with a quote from Teilhard's *The Mass on the World* (*La Messe sur le Monde*), a version of which was written in 1923 near the northern border with Mongolia, where Teilhard was participating in a scientific expedition:

> Radiant Word, blazing Power, you who mold the manifold so as to breathe life into it, I pray you, lay on us those your hands—powerful, considerate, omnipresent.

The pope's mention of Teilhard caused a bit of a stir among reporters and Vatican watchers, because Teilhard's writings were placed under a Vatican *monitum* in 1962 (renewed in 1981, just in case) for "dangerous ambiguities and grave errors." Fans have hoped for years that Pope Francis would remove any Vatican warnings from Teilhard's writings and rehabilitate the theologian/scientist. In 2017, after all, scholars from the Vatican's Pontifical Council for Culture itself noted Teilhard's "prophetic vision," and four different popes—Paul VI, John Paul II, Benedict XVI, and Francis—have referenced his writings (including, most recently, in Francis's *Laudato Si'*).

The renowned (or notorious, depending on whom you're talking to) Jesuit priest was born in 1881 in France and entered the Society of Jesus in 1899. The forced exile of the Jesuits from France in 1902 meant that he completed most of his studies in England and taught for three years at a Jesuit high school in Egypt. Ordained in 1911, he spent several years studying paleontology (including work on the dig that supposedly discovered "Piltdown Man," though the discovery was later discounted) before being drafted into the army in World War I, where he served as a stretcher-bearer, an experience reflected in some of the images in *The Mass on the World*.

In 1923, Teilhard traveled to China on a scientific expedition and completed the text for *The Mass on the World* that Pope Francis referred to in 2023 in Mongolia; he would return to China repeatedly over the next twenty-five years. His scientific work did not always endear him to his superiors. His work on evolutionary theory drew the attention of both his Jesuit superiors and the Holy Office, the precursor to today's mostly defanged Dicastery for the Doctrine of the Faith, and Teilhard was ordered to sign six statements on points where his thought appeared to conflict with traditional church teaching.

As the well-known Teilhard scholar Thomas M. King, S.J.,

once noted, "Teilhard was striving for sanctity by working in science, and this effort would require a new understanding of what it means to be holy." Once it became clear to him that he would not be allowed to publish or teach during his lifetime, he accepted a research position with a scientific foundation in New York in 1951.

In recent years, scholars have been divided about what some have identified as racist and eugenicist passages in Teilhard's work on the biological and spiritual evolution of humanity; in the summer of 2023, the scholars John P. Slattery and Juan V. Fernández de la Gala published an exchange on the subject in *America*. "There is considerable room for debate as to the extent to which Teilhard's racial and eugenic ideas affected his positive theological contributions," Slattery wrote. "However, it seems prudent that any significant promotion of his ideas—like a centennial celebration of his works—should at least mention the contemporary challenges of his views on race and eugenics, if for no other reason than to pay respect to the millions of people who suffered the consequences of racist science and eugenics."

Fernández de la Gala argued that Teilhard's focus was on a spiritual purification of humanity, not biological engineering. "I have not found evidence at all of any Teilhardian support of biological eugenics, supremacist ideas, or racial discrimination. To the contrary, the evolutionary way to the Omega Point that he invites us to is first a noospheric revolution that renews and reconstitutes evolution, endows it with a purpose, and removes it from the brutal blindness of chance," Fernández de la Gala wrote. "Finally, it is a spiritual revolution along the lines of the happy utopia of the kingdom of God as preached by Jesus of Nazareth."

Teilhard died in New York City on Easter Sunday, April

10, 1955, and is buried on the grounds of the former novitiate of the New York Province of the Society of Jesus in Hyde Park, N.Y. Though the Culinary Institute of America (a different C.I.A., not the one the Jesuits control) has owned the property for more than fifty years, visitors can still request a key to the cemetery gate to visit Teilhard's grave.

Much of Teilhard's fame came posthumously, particularly with the publication of his major works *The Divine Milieu* and *The Phenomenon of Man*. Teilhard is remembered most for his concepts of the social evolution of humanity, which could be partially directed by humanity itself (transcending physical evolution); the convergence of all creation toward a moment of omniscience and unity of consciousness, which he called the "Omega Point" and identified with the *Logos* of Christ; and the integral relationship between humanity and the rest of matter in a constantly evolving universe.

That summary is painfully inadequate to the person or the subject. But more can be found in the work of those who championed his work, among them the famed theologian of the Second Vatican Council, Henri de Lubac, S.J., whose 1965 *Teilhard de Chardin: The Man and His Meaning* followed by four more books on Teilhard in the coming years; other fans of his work included Joseph Ratzinger, the future Pope Benedict XVI, who wrote of Teilhard's Christology in his *Introduction to Christianity* that "[i]t must be regarded as an important service of Teilhard de Chardin's that he rethought these ideas from the angle of the modern view of the world."

Flannery O'Connor also quoted Teilhard for a 1961 short story that later became the title of a collection, "Everything That Rises Must Converge." But probably Teilhard's most famous quote comes from his 1936 essay, "The Evolution of Chastity":

Someday, after mastering the winds, the waves, the tides and gravity, we shall harness for God the energies of love, and then, for a second time in the history of the world, man will have discovered fire.

I had an unexpected personal moment of connection with Teilhard in October 2014, while I was departing the subway at 231st and Broadway in New York City. There I came across a street vendor selling secondhand books and magazines. Square in the middle of the table, among all those Harlequin romances and old issues of *Time*, there it was: his *The Phenomenon of Man*.

Perhaps a far more exacting authority than the Vatican had rehabilitated Teilhard de Chardin: The Bronx.

17

WALKER PERCY
Style and Snark

The sixtieth anniversary of Walker Percy's novel *The Moviegoer* in 2022 was occasion enough for me to look up reviews of Walker Percy's novel that won the National Book Award in 1962. What I found instead was surprising: Percy's name appeared in more than a few Catholic magazines in the years before, but not because of *The Moviegoer*. It turns out that Percy had been writing short pieces for different magazines for years. His first essay was in *Commonweal* in 1956.

Sometimes Percy wrote book reviews, sometimes articles on sociological or religious topics, sometimes social commentary. The best find of all, however, was his 1974 *America* book review of Paul Horgan's *Approaches to Writing*. Once upon a time, Paul Horgan was an even more famous writer than Percy, having won the Pulitzer Prize for Fiction twice—even if his name has faded somewhat in recent decades.

Percy's review of Horgan's text is its own delightful primer on how to write, full of pithy observations about the craft and not without a fair dose of Percy snark.

"Pay attention, says Horgan, to such humble mechanics of the craft as spelling, punctuation, grammar, syntax. Spelling!

Groans from the sophomore in Creative Writing already out-Faulknering Faulkner—Horgan is a nag. No, Horgan is right," Percy wrote. "Writing is a craft like any other. Writers and carpenters had better have respect for the workaday tools of the trade, the feel of the wood under the thumb."

"Writing for a living is, for some reason or other, the only occupation to which people still ascribe a species of demonism," he continued. "This state of affairs is probably the last legacy of 100 years of bad romanticism, the writer possessed, the writer post-epileptic."

"Most writers, especially fiction writers, have their little eccentricities, lining up pencil and paper a certain way, but these are less apt to be signs of madness than a very human anxiety to preserve what Horgan calls 'an induced and pro-tracted absentmindedness,'" Percy wrote. "Evelyn Waugh once reported that he thought Graham Greene a little strange because he had to run out in the street and wait for a car to pass with a certain combination of numbers on the license plate before he could get to work. But Waugh of all people should have had sympathy for the quailings, twitches, and fits which are apt to befall a man trying to write a good sentence." *Zing!*

Percy, who died in 1990, wrote four more novels and more than a dozen nonfiction works, including a harsh mockery of the self-help movement, *Lost in the Cosmos: The Last Self-Help Book*, and a book of essays put together a decade after his death by his longtime friend and biographer, Patrick Samway, S.J., *Signposts in a Strange Land*. Among his readers, Percy tends to attract strange bedfellows, as likely to appeal to a reader of *Commonweal* as a reader of the *Wanderer* or similarly themed traditionalist Catholic journals.

Samway eventually wrote a biography of him, *Walker*

Percy: A Life, in 1997. Both Samway and Percy were published by Farrar, Straus & Giroux, the venerable publishing house that has featured an intimidating roster of accomplished writers over the years, from John Berryman to Susan Sontag, Joan Didion, Philip Roth, Tom Wolfe, Jonathan Franzen, Robert Lowell, Bernard Malamud, Jeffrey Eugenides, Alice McDermott, and Paul Elie. Oh, and Thomas Merton and Flannery O'Connor too.

How did the editors gather so much talent in one place? Editor Robert Giroux offered a hint: "The most sobering of all publishing lessons," he once said, is that "a great book is often ahead of its time, and the trick is how to keep it afloat until the times catch up with it." Percy, for example, was a medical doctor who had been working on drafts of *The Moviegoer* for years before Knopf snatched up the manuscript.

While the cosmopolitan and debonair Roger W. Straus Jr. was the public face of FSG, his secret weapon was Giroux (whose papers are archived at Loyola New Orleans through the efforts of Samway). "A native of New Jersey who attended the Jesuit-run Regis High School in Manhattan, Giroux was confidant and editor to T. S. Eliot and Thomas Merton, among others," wrote Maurice Timothy Reidy in a 2014 review of Boris Kachka's history of Farrar, Straus & Giroux, *Hothouse*. "He helped bring *Seven Storey Mountain* to fruition and was among the first to read *Catcher in the Rye*, a book his boss at Harcourt, Brace turned down."

There was one book, however, that escaped Giroux's grasp. "While at Harcourt, he published Jack Kerouac's first book, though he didn't know what to make of a second novel the mercurial writer delivered to his offices on a single roll of paper," Reidy wrote. "When Giroux told him they would need separate pages for editing, Kerouac reacted with indignation and stormed off. *On the Road* was published by Viking six years later."

That brings us full circle. Because having read Walker Percy's thoughts on writing, I have no doubt that he was thrilled to work with Giroux—and would have absolutely despised sharing catalog pages with *On the Road*.

18

John Kennedy Toole
An Ignatian Worldview

The rise of "prestige television" over the last several decades has been paralleled by a rise in our acceptance in popular culture of the antihero: a protagonist who is compelling and engrossing as a character but deeply flawed (or openly villainous) in a way that puts him or her beyond the pale of society. Tony Soprano and Walter White are the two classic examples, and recent TV shows like *Killing Eve* center on characters—Eve and Villanelle—whose moral compass has no true north.

It's not all new, of course. We've always loved our gangsters and our cowboy rustlers, and much of the tension of American fiction is found in the question of whether an appealing character will "break bad." But it seems more prevalent these days. One author who presaged this era was John Kennedy Toole, whose posthumous 1980 novel, *A Confederacy of Dunces,* introduced us to one of the funniest and most outrageous antiheroes of any era: Ignatius J. Reilly.

A lonely, oversized, and unemployed misanthrope who lives with his mother, Irene, but imagines himself a wise and misunderstood sage, Ignatius J. Reilly is one of many technicolor characters in Toole's novel, including the city of New Orleans itself (which now has a statue of Ignatius on Canal Street). Through his self-valorizing diary entries as well as his letters to an equally antisocial love interest, Myrna Minkoff, Ignatius offers social commentary and outrageous fantasies about his role as a modern-day Boethius who will restore to harmony the chaotic world in which he lives—especially if it means he doesn't have to work very hard or moderate his own huge appetites.

Ignatius shouldn't arouse our sympathies: he is cruel to his mother, rude to almost everyone he meets, and comically lacking in self-reflection or humility. And yet he has charmed four decades of readers since the novel's publication in 1980. Kevin Spinale, S.J., was straightforward in his endorsement of the book in 2020: "I think that we need this novel *now more than ever.*"

But why? Spinale admits there's much about the book and its protagonist to dislike. The book is such an equal-opportunity offender in terms of racial and sexual stereo-types that probably only Martin Amis could get away with it today, and indeed there is much of John Self from *Money* in the protagonist. "[B]oth Ignatius J. Reilly and John Kennedy Toole, Ignatius' creator, are utterly beyond the pale," Spinale writes. "Utterly. Not only is some of the language and many of the characters of the novel unacceptable and offensive, but the book's main character resides so absurdly beyond the pale that he aligns himself passionately with the 'geometry and theology' of the medieval period."

At the same time, he argues, "I think we also need comedy—actual laugh-out-loud, wonderfully thoughtful, uniquely creative comedy. Comedy that helps us be more human, less afraid, and less serious about ourselves. Now, we need Ignatius

Jacques Reilly and this warmly funny novel to help keep us reflective and hopeful."

A moment when Ignatius finds brief employment running a hot-dog cart is emblematic of both the humor and the absurdity of *Dunces*. Here is Ignatius's diary entry for the time:

> At first I thought I might have found a surrogate father in the czar of sausage, the mogul of meat. But his resentment and jealousy of me are increasing daily; no doubt, they will ultimately overwhelm him and destroy his mind. The grandeur of my physique, the complexity of my worldview, the decency and taste implicit in my carriage, the grace with which I function in the mire of today's world—all of these at once confuse and astound Clyde. Now he has relegated me to working in the French Quarter, an area which houses every vice that man has ever conceived in his wildest aberrations, including, I would imagine, several modern variants made possible through the wonders of modern science.

Hard not to laugh—but also hard not to think *My God this is what Donald Trump would be like if he were poor and Catholic.* The narcissism, the megalomania, the unwarranted self-regard. It doesn't just occur in fiction. We laugh at and with Ignatius, but we also recognize that even the most comic of antiheroes has real-life parallels.

A Confederacy of Dunces won the Pulitzer Prize for Fiction in 1981, a stunning turnabout for a novel whose publication itself was a bit of a miracle. Its author, John Kennedy Toole, struggled to complete his doctorate in literature or hold steady work; he had shopped the initial manuscript of *Dunces* to a commercial publisher before despairing of it ever seeing publication. Suffering from depression, he committed suicide in 1969 at the age of thirty-one. According to his mother, her son's depression was caused partly by his inability to find a home for the book. She took it upon herself to find a publisher and spent the next decade trying.

She finally gave the manuscript to Walker Percy, who was teaching at Loyola New Orleans. Percy was not impressed at first, but then began reading—and couldn't put it down. After a few years, he found an academic press—Louisiana State University Press—to publish the book. A year later, it had sold 45,000 copies and won the Pulitzer.

Why isn't there a movie version of *A Confederacy of Dunces*? There is a legend the project is cursed (among the actors proposed for the role of Ignatius are three who died prematurely: John Belushi, John Candy, and Chris Farley). But more likely every attempt to bring it to the silver screen has foundered because the novel is simply unfilmable. It is neither farce nor satire, and its humor comes from Ignatius's pen as much as from his bumbling exploits around New Orleans. No actor alive or dead—sorry, not even Nick Offerman—could possibly capture Ignatius's personality.

To quote John Waters when his own attempt failed: "How can a movie ever live up to that book?"

19

KIRSTIN VALDEZ QUADE
The Pursuit of Grace

"This year Amadeo Padilla is Jesus."

This opening line in a 2009 story in the *New Yorker* introduced the larger literary world to the fiction of Kirstin Valdez Quade. That Amadeo Padilla in "The Five Wounds" is also the local ne'er-do-well, an absent father with multiple DUIs and more scars on his body than jobs on his resume, also revealed Valdez Quade's remarkable ability to work within and around religious symbols and metaphors in her work.

Padilla, readers soon found out, is just playing Jesus in his town's yearly reenactment of the crucifixion of Jesus. Nevertheless, he ultimately asks not for a faked crucifixion, but for real nails to be used on his hands and his feet. Jesus, his savior, was convicted and executed as a criminal. Padilla, a criminal, asks to share in the literal sufferings of Jesus.

Valdez Quade included "The Five Wounds" in her 2015 short-story collection, *Night at the Fiestas,* which earned plaudits from the National Book Foundation, the *New York Times,* and the *San Francisco Chronicle*, among others. She then expanded and adapted the story for her eponymous debut novel in 2021, another award-winning effort that author Colm Tóibín praised for its "luminous and memorable detail."

In addition to the novel's perfect pacing, he wrote, each scene was made with tact and care: "Kirstin Valdez Quade, by concentrating on the truth of small moments, has brought a whole world into focus."

Valdez Quade was raised in rural New Mexico (the setting for *The Five Wounds* and most of her stories) and credits her grandmother and great-grandmother for the sense of Catholicity in her work. "I consider myself Catholic," she told the novelist and critic Jenny Shank in a 2018 interview. "That history, that tradition, feels very central to my understanding of my family history and my place in the world. On the other hand, there are a lot of ways in which I feel that it's a pretty inhospitable religion for me. I think that's another tension that I keep returning to. What does it mean for me to love this religion that I don't always feel wants me?"

Regardless of that tension, the incarnational sense of Catholic fiction that David Tracy and Andrew Greeley have both written about in the past is immediately recognizable in Valdez Quade's work. "Jesus Christ's paschal pain is everywhere in *The Five Wounds*," wrote Kevin Spinale, S.J., in a 2021 essay on *The Five Wounds*. Indeed, in the visceral reenactment of the passion of Jesus that bookends the novel, Spinale notes, Amadeo Padilla "recognizes a further truth: '*To feel a little of what Christ felt.* Tío Tíve said that over a year ago. And what Christ felt was love. Amadeo doesn't know how he lost track of this. Love: both gift and challenge.'"

Another short story from *Night at the Fiestas*, "Ordinary Sins," takes place in a parish office, where a woman partially based on Valdez Quade's grandmother keeps the parish running in the midst of the sacred and the quotidian. For the priests and the lay employees alike, the daily work is by turns boring and sublime.

"I'm interested in priests because they are dealing with the most sacred and important moments in their parishioners' lives, and they're this intermediary between their parishioners and God," Valdez Quade told Shank in 2018. "On the other hand, it's a job that they have to do, day in and day out. And presumably there are office politics and all kinds of tedium. I love the juxtaposition of the everyday tedium of the job and the holiness of it."

Some of Valdez Quade's other short stories, like "Christina the Astonishing (1150–1224)," also explore the parallels between holiness and everyday struggles, as with the title character's unacknowledged mental illness in that story.

What does Valdez Quade herself think about how religious her stories and characters can be, even when the theme is not religion at all? "I always feel a little bit like I'm maybe not equal to the task," she told Shank of the many Catholic and Christian publications that have praised her work within the broader literary reviews she receives. "I think one of the reasons I continue to write about these themes is because my own thoughts about it are still uncertain. I'm still figuring out what I think and I believe. So I don't always feel like I'm the best person to actually talk about it."

Her readers seem to disagree about that. "What I continually recognize in Valdez Quade's work is the pursuit of grace," wrote Liam Callanan in a 2017 essay in *America* on faith and fiction. "Grace is often out of reach of her characters—but only ever just out of reach." It is a testament to Valdez Quade's skill, he writes, "that engaged readers come to see the truth even as her characters do not."

20

JOHN IRVING
Making the Miraculous Real

There was a seven-year gap since the publication of his last novel, and five years since he announced that he was well on his way to completing his next opus, then titled *Darkness as a Bride*. Other than a surprise appearance as a book reviewer in the *New York Times* in August, John Irving had kept his fans waiting for quite a while. But it finally arrived: in the fall of 2023, John Irving published *The Last Chairlift*.

The new novel, his fifteenth, features a family as quirky as any in Irving's corpus. Veterans of Irving might prepare themselves for unexpected pregnancy, a fatherless son, the full gamut of sexual expression, ghosts and avatars, and—one can only assume, since this is John Irving—some wrestling and some infidelity and some bears.

Irving is suddenly eighty years old, a bit of a shock considering he has always appeared quite youthful. His early novels, including *Setting Free the Bears* (1968) and *The Water-Method Man* (1972), earned some critical acclaim but modest commercial success. It was not until his fourth novel, *The World according to Garp* (1978), that Irving became an international phenomenon—compared to Charles Dickens (one of his own favorite authors), featured on the cover of *Time* and honored with the National Book Award for Fiction in 1980. A popular movie adaptation of *Garp* starring Robin Williams, Glenn Close, and John Lithgow further introduced Irving to new audiences.

Garp is a sprawling novel at over six hundred pages, but quite readable; when I first picked it up I couldn't put it down—except to cry at the *echt* Irving moments when an act of bravery or ardor or violence forcibly and dramatically altered the lives of his characters in abrupt ways.

The years following brought *The Hotel New Hampshire, The Cider House Rules* (more about that in a minute), *A Prayer for Owen Meany, A Son of the Circus,* and five more. The novels have become more and more autobiographical in many ways, and some would have benefited from a diet: *The Last Chairlift* is perhaps his heftiest tome at 912 pages.

I interviewed Irving in December 2017 in Toronto, where he was writing drafts of what would become *The Last Chairlift* in longhand on yellow legal pads. Irving's most recent novel at the time, 2015's *Avenue of Mysteries*, had featured a protagonist named Juan Diego whose sister received visions of the Virgin Mary. Throughout the novel (much of it set in Mexico), statues weep and the supernatural repeatedly intrudes on reality. Other characters included a Jesuit scholastic and a slum priest.

Was there something of a Catholic sensibility to his writing? I wondered. Yes and no. "What I wanted to do in this novel was to make the miraculous very real, while the institution of the church itself is severely criticized," Irving told me. "It is impossible to spend even as much time as I spent in Mexico and in those basilicas, those cathedrals, those churches, in the presence of those various virgins, and the many people you see on their knees asking something of them—it is impossible not to feel the strength of faith in those virgins so many people have."

At the same time, Irving has long been a vocal supporter of legal abortion, a major theme in *The Cider House Rules*, and is vehement in his criticism of the Catholic Church for its opposition to abortion. While he found Pope Francis a nice change from previous popes, "I remain dubious when [Pope Francis] has said that he believes we, the church in general, have emphasized too much the gay marriage issue and the abortion rights issue—which so many, as he admits, good and practicing Catholics are on the liberal side of."

"Perhaps one day, if not in my lifetime or yours, some relenting on the gay marriage issue strikes me as more likely than any giving-in on the abortion issue. Which, especially in Third World countries, puts so many poor and disadvantaged women in a minority and subservient role," he continued. "I would not want to be born a girl in a Third World economy where the Catholic Church is calling the shots."

At the same time, it is clear that faith (or its absence) plays an important role in Irving's fiction, even if his characters and plots almost always serve to resist or complicate the role of organized religion. Irving, who was raised a Congregationalist but does not belong to any organized religious denomination, writes characters who, like Flannery O'Connor's American South, seem somehow God-haunted.

"In school and university I took every academic course in religion and the history of religions. Because I was always interested in the power of belief and what it was that people believed in, without feeling that I much resembled a believer myself," Irving said. "In the same vein, I would say that I'm often as resistant to the confidence of atheists as I am to the confidence of true believers."

"I find the most outspoken atheists and true believers also have in common the desire to bring you into their fold. It is not sufficient for them to have their beliefs and to allow you to have yours. It is necessary that they bring you on board. Pot smokers are a lot like that too."

In a review of *A Prayer for Owen Meany* for the *Washington Post* in 1989, Stephen King put it another way. Irving, he said, "writes novels in the unglamourous but effective way Babe Ruth used to hit home runs. . . . He does not dance, duck, dodge, or beat around the burning bush; he simply walks up to the subject of divinity and briskly smites it, hip and thigh."

21

Francis X. Talbot
The Meanest Editor in the World

In the fall of 1932, a new monthly literary magazine, the *American Spectator*, debuted in the United States with an impressive roster of editors, including George Jean Nathan, Theodore Dreiser, James Branch Cabell, and Eugene O'Neill. The prominent syndicated newspaper columnist O. O. McIntyre wrote that "New York's literati are in a furious flutter over the last word in literary high-hatting," reporting that contributors to the new journal would include William Faulkner, Ernest Hemingway, James Joyce, and Sinclair Lewis, among other literary giants.

A few weeks after the journal's debut, Francis X. Talbot, S.J., the literary editor of *America*, reviewed it. In perhaps the first example of headline clickbait, the title of his review was a spicy one: "The World's Worst Magazine." What followed was a florid, funny, fierce jeremiad against the new enterprise.

"Now I would not be the one to say that our esteemed contemporary, the *Commonweal*, is any worse than *America*; hence, that weekly is ruled out. Not even our deluded contemporaries, the *New Republic* and the *Nation*, are now the worst," Talbot declared. As for the *American Spectator*'s editors and contributors, "almost all of them are dull and wordy propagandists for animal sexuality, social promiscuity, and godlessness."

He could go on. He *did* go on:

> These are humorless men, overwhelmed by the futility of all about them, blinded to the light which makes life livable. They are sad men who have exhausted the material pleasures of the world and in whose souls the instinct of hope is dead. They are the rebels against all that the generations of normal men have found to be wisdom, and they writhe and twist in the trammels of their own pride and folly.

(I hasten to note that the *American Spectator* of which he wrote, which failed in 1936, has no connection to the politically conservative journal the *American Spectator* that exists today, and which I have only thrice called The World's Worst Magazine.)

In 1934, Talbot commented on James Joyce's *Ulysses* and a recent court case in the United States that had declared the book was not obscene. Talbot didn't agree with the judge on the novel's merits:

> The book was written in a new technique, in a pseudo-English, of words that were sometimes normal, sometimes foreign, sometimes archaic, sometimes merely a succession of letters, meaningless and inane. Many of the words were scummy, scrofulous, putrid, like excrement of the mind. The words are listed in the dictionary, but never in the writings or on the tongue of anyone except the insane, or the lowest human dregs.

Describing the protagonists of *Ulysses*, Talbot had more to say. "What they and the other characters thought and imagined, what trivialities, what nonsense, what drunken dreams, hallucinations, eroticisms, vulgarities, blasphemies, silliness, malice, and the like streamed through their consciousness and unconsciousness is what James Joyce labored for seven years to transmit to 768 closely printed pages," he wrote. "Because of the filthiness that whirled in the stream, those seeking to be pornographicized exclaimed what excitement. And the man with a sound brain and a sound heart exclaimed what twaddle and what rot."

Who was this wordsmith, and what gave him such an extraordinarily cheeky literary style? Born in 1889, Francis X. Talbot entered the Society of Jesus in 1906 and was ordained a priest in 1921. He became literary editor of *America* in 1923, a position he held until his appointment as editor in chief in 1936. Talbot also founded or assisted with the creation of an extraordinary number of journals and literary societies, including *Theological Studies*, *Thought*, the Catholic Book Club, the Catholic Poetry Society of America, and the Catholic Library Association.

His tenure as editor in chief was not without its troubles—Talbot's strong antipathy for communism led the magazine to offer support to Spain's dictator, Francisco Franco. "He tried to communicate to the contents of the Review itself and its discussion of current issues the dramatic, crusading spirit which its exterior form then symbolized," wrote John LaFarge, S.J., in a 1953 obituary of Talbot. "This tactic worked effectively where the topic lent itself to black-and-white treatment, but did not succeed equally well where more careful analysis was required." Talbot stepped down after eight years at the helm of *America* and was succeeded by LaFarge.

Talbot's other writings are extraordinary both for their eloquence and their frank truculence: he suffered no fools and, it seems, little self-doubt. A ten-part series on writing in 1933 and 1934 began with "The Agony of Writing," in which he wrote that "sometimes it is a rather miserable life, this profession of letters, and sometimes it intoxicates one so that he could sing for the joy of being an author." Like many of his writings, his advice in that column displayed some of the sheer pleasure he took in being a wordsmith:

> One who is actively engaged in the painful pursuit of literature, is always engaged in it, every moment, and is never entirely free of it. He need not necessarily be on the lookout for material; he cannot avoid or escape the material, for it forces itself on him. . . . He is never immune from a good idea, or a good scene, or a good phrase, or a good plot.

Such craft, he wrote in a later column, is nothing less than "the expression of a man's soul." Every writer must have "a feeling for words, a sensitiveness toward them, a kind of tender respect for them," he wrote, adding:

> He should be aware of their connotations and associations, he should see images and pictures in each of them, he should be able to taste their flavor, to savor of them, he should know their strength and their pungency and their potency and their quietude, he should be able to measure instinctively their appropriateness to what he writes and for whom he writes. . . . Each word is a test by which the writer is judged.

Talbot later served as president of Loyola College in Baltimore (now Loyola University Maryland) from 1947 to 1950; he then worked in various capacities as an archivist, retreat director, and parish priest until his death in 1953, continuing his own writing all the while. His books included *Saint among Savages: The Life of St. Isaac Jogues* (1935) and *Saint among the Hurons: The Life of Jean de Brébeuf* (1949).

In his 1953 obituary of Talbot, LaFarge wrote less about Talbot's literary output or fiery temperament than of another quality seen by his peers:

> There was always much to say about "F. X. T.," whether you took him as a fine scholar, a natural leader of men, or as a truly saintly, apostolic priest. If you try to describe a great and colorful personality to those for whom he is but a name, there is little you can do save select some master epithet that in crude fashion may help to sum him up. In this instance the word does seem to come to hand: it is magnanimity.

Not a bad sendoff—but I bet if "F.X.T." had been allowed to write his own obituary, it would have been slightly more colorful.

22

J. R. R. TOLKIEN
The "Long Defeat," the Final Victory

The weekend of September 2, 2023, marked both the forty-ninth anniversary of the death of J. R. R. Tolkien at the age of eighty-one and the release of the first two episodes of a Tolkien-inspired TV series, *The Rings of Power*. Though not adapted from Tolkien's writings in any strict sense, the series takes place in the fantasy world of Middle-earth in which his famous novels *The Hobbit* and the three *The Lord of the Rings* books were set, and is imagined as a prequel to those storylines.

Not everyone was pleased by the new series, either because it lacked the memorable characters and storylines of Tolkien's other works or because the creators dared to depict hobbits as something other than lily-white (I'm not making this up) or because it was not slavishly faithful to the fantasy world Tolkien created. And if Elon Musk is to be believed, J. R. R. Tolkien "is turning in his grave" because of the way male characters are portrayed in *The Rings of Power*. Why so much *Sturm und Drang* over a TV show?

Because if you like J. R. R. Tolkien's writings, *you love J. R. R. Tolkien's writings*. And you have opinions. His fans exemplify the etymology of the word: *fanaticus* (usually more in the "zealous, affected by enthusiasm" sense than "insane, enthusiastic, inspired by a god," but not always). These are the folks who learn Elvish, who name their kids Bilbo or Gandalf or Galadriel. A professor in graduate school once caught me scrolling online in class; after a moment's wrath, he admitted that when he was in school, he occupied himself during many a boring lecture by writing out the genealogies of the kings of Middle-earth. That's a fan.

Tolkien himself was as fascinating as the tales he wrought, a linguistic genius who spoke or read upward of thirty languages (and invented several more), who fought in the trenches in World War I but also translated the Book of Jonah for the *New Jerusalem Bible*. A university professor for decades, he was a key member of "The Inklings," an informal literary club that included C. S. Lewis, Owen Barfield, and Charles Williams and met weekly from roughly 1933 through 1949 to discuss each other's work. C. S. Lewis, among the best-known writers of the set, attributed his embrace of Christianity to Tolkien's influence.

"They were not especially well-traveled or urbane. They came from ordinary middle-class families. Except perhaps for Williams, none was particularly known for personal charisma," wrote Rachel Lu of the Inklings in 2022. "On some level, the Inklings were just a clique of fusty old English intellectuals, possessed of none of the savvy instincts that we associate today with 'influencers.'" But "somehow these men transcended their own times and circumstances, translating Christian ideas into a language that everyone wanted to hear."

There was always a stratum of British literary society that disdained the Inklings. After Humphrey Carpenter published a study of the group, *The Inklings*, in 1978, Albert F.

Reddy, S.J., commented that he "was surprised by the critics chosen by the *Sunday Times* and the *Observer* to review it. Neither John Carey nor Philip Toynbee made the least effort to conceal his dislike for the group. . . . The Inklings, it seemed, even in death could still excite strong feelings, producing angry critics as well as devoted admirers."

Both Lu and Reddy delved into a central element of Tolkien's life that may have contributed to a certain suspicion of him among the literati: his Catholic faith. In his collected letters (published in 1981), Tolkien wrote repeatedly of his devotion to the Blessed Sacrament, the importance of prayer (including prayers of lament), and the connection between his faith and his fiction. In a letter to a friend, Tolkien noted that "*The Lord of the Rings* is of course a fundamentally religious and Catholic work; unconsciously so at first, but consciously in the revision. That is why I have not put in, or have cut out, practically all references to anything like 'religion,' to cults or practices, in the imaginary world. For the religious element is absorbed into the story and the symbolism."

Tolkien always had a largely pessimistic view of the world—perhaps both because of his experiences in the trenches and because he lost both parents in childhood—but he saw that tendency as of a piece with his faith, rather than contrary to it. Reddy noted "Tolkien's passion for perfection, which prevented him from publishing more than he did, along with his good-naturedness, his sense of fun, his love of nature and his dedication to his family." However, he wrote, the book "also presents a man whose view of life was deeply pessimistic (as a boy he lost both his parents) and who suffered recurring periods of depression."

Tolkien himself admitted as much. In 2020, Jessica Hooten Wilson noted that "Tolkien himself did not see history as a series of worldly victories." She quotes one of his letters to this effect:

> Actually I am a Christian and indeed a Roman Catholic, so that I do not expect "history" to be anything but a "long defeat"—though it contains . . . some samples or glimpses of final victory.

Readers of *The Lord of the Rings* will certainly recognize all those themes: the miraculous Lembas bread that keeps Frodo and Samwise alive on their journey; the sense of the world inevitably devolving into a slaughter of innocents; the frailty of Frodo in the crucial moments before the final victory over evil. Tolkien's fantasy world was in many ways a direct reflection of his understanding of reality.

Amazon executives might not care about all that, but they had plenty of other reasons to greenlight *The Rings of Power*. Between them, *The Hobbit*, *The Lord of the Rings* books, and *The Silmarillion* have sold more than six hundred million copies; in theaters, *The Hobbit* and *The Lord of the Rings* movies have together grossed more than $2 billion. There's a lot of fans out there—including Pope Francis.

23

Iris Murdoch
The Virtue of "Unselfing"

She was banned from studying in the United States as a young woman because she had been a communist in college. She was Irish-born but rarely returned home and once described herself as "unsentimental about Ireland." She married an Oxford professor but had romantic affairs with both men and women throughout their marriage. Her novels treated subjects considered beyond the pale by many reviewers—and certainly so for Catholic literary sensibilities in the 1950s and 1960s. An atheist, she described religion as "no longer sustainable" in the modern age.

An unlikely candidate to become a popular fiction writer for the religious set—but that was Iris Murdoch.

Murdoch first started to garner literary notice with her 1957 novel *The Sandcastle*, her third. Numerous positive mentions followed throughout the next three decades; her 1968 novel, *The Nice and the Good,* was reviewed in *America* by William B. Hill, S.J., who wrote that the book, "though filled with incident, including murder and perilous adventure, still manages to be profound—perhaps Miss Murdoch's best to date." Father Hill reviewed 1972's *An Accidental Man* as well, praising Murdoch for "characters in sprawling abundance, most of them perfectly limned."

In a 1973 review of Murdoch's *The Black Prince*, James R. Lindroth noted Murdoch's "enduring concern" about solipsism and narcissism as dominant themes in modern life; "unlike many of her contemporaries who do no more than confirm man's despair, she reaffirms love as a force capable of shattering the shell of self." *The Black Prince*, Lindroth wrote, "marks a further step in the artistic development of one of England's most impressive authors."

In a long 1974 roundup of "The Year's Best in Paperbacks," Paul C. Doherty praised Murdoch's *A Fairly Honorable Defeat*, "in which the only character who can consistently respond to the events of the story with charity, intelligence, and dignity is the homosexual hero, Axel, and yet Axel must hide his true feelings from all but his closest friends." Doherty linked Murdoch's latest effort to E. M. Forster's novel *Maurice*, first written in 1913 but not published until 1971 because the title character was gay.

A 1980 review by James Gaffney treated Murdoch's nonfiction text *The Fire and the Sun: Why Plato Banished the Artists.* Calling Murdoch "one of my favorite modern fiction writers as well as one of my favorite modern philosophers," Gaffney gave the book high praise, writing that it "sums up vast traces of Platonic thought so well that it could serve as either an introduction to Plato or a source of new insight." In 1983, Samuel Coale praised Murdoch's *The Philosopher's Pupil* as a "fat, dazzling novel" that "demonstrates Murdoch's penchant for allegory."

Those three decades of approbation weren't the end of Catholic media's fascination with Murdoch's life and works, and just four years ago, James K. A. Smith penned a long essay, "The Moral Vision of Iris Murdoch," after the publication of Gary Browning's *Why Iris Murdoch Matters*, in which he wrote:

> At the heart of Murdoch's moral vision is what she calls "unselfing," something surely worth revisiting in the age of the selfie. As one might guess, this amounts to finding a way out of the claustrophobia of our self-regard by answering a call from outside.

Murdoch was born in 1919 in Dublin to a Protestant family, but her family moved to London when she was an infant. After studying classics and philosophy at Oxford and Cambridge, she taught philosophy for many years at Oxford. In 1956, she married John Bayley, an Oxford English professor and novelist, though their long-lasting union was recognized by both partners as an open marriage. (The 2001 film *Iris*, starring Kate Winslet and Dame Judi Dench as Murdoch, was based on Bayley's memoirs about their marriage and Murdoch's eventual death in 1999 from Alzheimer's disease.)

Though Murdoch is remembered most often on this side of the pond as a fiction writer, her twenty-six novels (and several plays) were all published only after *Sartre: Romantic Rationalist*, her 1953 book that introduced many English-language readers to the philosophy of Jean-Paul Sartre for the first time—and Sartre's themes of alienation and solipsism in modern life certainly found their way into many of her works of fiction. As a philosopher, Murdoch is noted for her work on the cultivation of virtue and the search for meaning in modern life.

Murdoch, noted Smith in his essay, objected to the separation of ethics from personal development. "Ethics left in the hands of philosophers became one more epistemic puzzle.

The problem of the moral life was construed as either ignorance or paralysis in the face of moral dilemmas. But Murdoch knew this was all a smokescreen," wrote Smith. "The source of our moral problems is not that we do not know enough; the problem is us. 'In the moral life the enemy is the fat relentless ego,' she wryly remarked."

Murdoch became more of a novelist than a philosopher as the years went by, though the two vocations always seemed linked. She was awarded the Booker Prize in 1978 for *The Sea, the Sea*, and was made a Dame of the British Empire by Queen Elizabeth II in 1987. That same year, she won the Royal Society Literary Award. Her novels were often sprawling affairs, full of multiple characters and plot twists, but a common theme was love in all its forms—and all its possible modern permutations.

"For Murdoch, love's pageant was by turns chimerical, alchemical, and miraculous," wrote Gerald T. Cobb, S.J., in a 2002 review of *Iris Murdoch*, a biography by Peter J. Conradi. "Her fiction implicitly argues that one must be something of a philosopher to be a true lover, and conversely that one must be something of a lover to be a profound philosopher."

Much of that fiction—about alienated people searching for love in all the right and wrong places—remains pertinent today. "We in the United States might not have been ready for Murdoch in her lifetime," Smith wrote. "She wrote in and for a post-Christian world that has only more recently become our shared experience. She wrote for a world that is now our milieu."

24

J. F. POWERS
Transcending Worldly Ambitions

What is worse, a sin of commission or one of omission? In the case of the obituary writers of the *New York Times* over the decades, the latter failings call out more loudly for repentance. Any survey of the accounts of lives of religious novelists is all the evidence you need. With what words would you bury Evelyn Waugh? The *Times* chose "Evelyn Waugh, Satirical Novelist, Is Dead at 62." His greatest triumph, *Brideshead Revisited,* is described as (not kidding) "a tragic recounting of the decline of a great English family."

J. F. Powers didn't fare much better. This finalist for the National Book Award in Fiction for 1957, the winner of that award in 1963, a writer hailed as a literary lion by everyone from Flannery O'Connor to Philip Roth to Mary Gordon to Frank O'Connor, was dispatched upon his death in 1999 with "J. F. Powers, 81, Dies; Wrote about Priests."

I suppose it's not entirely wrong: both of his novels (*Morte D'Urban* in 1962, *Wheat That Springeth Green* in 1988) and many of his short stories had priests as protagonists, and surely no American writer has ever captured the quotidian existence of parish priests better than Powers. But you wouldn't bury a writer with "Hemingway: Wrote about Drunks" nor "Melville: Wrote about a Whale." There's a sneer behind the headline, the passing regret that J. F. Powers didn't write about something more compelling.

Note how James Wood began his *New Yorker* essay on Powers in 2000 after the author's works were republished (they had all gone out of print) by the *New York Review of Books*: "Does anyone, really, like priests?" Wood noted that "it seems sadly likely that the combination of Powers's refined style, ironic pessimism, and chosen subject—priests and more priests—will eventually deal his work a second death."

What Wood and more than a few other critics over the years missed is that Powers's chosen subjects—in cassocks or nay—are inevitably All-American, and both his novels as well as many of the short stories are careful (and yes, ironically pessimistic) studies of American mid-century life and ambition. Father Urban and Father Joe (the protagonists of Powers's novels) are not saints or mystics; neither is even a pious man. Yes, they are holy in their own way, and Powers gives them worthy dénouements that befit a Gospel parable, but at heart they are midwestern American men who want a promotion in the corporation. A bigger church, their own parish, a more important position in their religious order; maybe, after a few beers, they have a fanciful thought or two of one day becoming a bishop.

Powers is in on the joke. The ambitions of both men—as well as of other priests in his short stories, as in the absolutely brilliant "Prince of Darkness"—are as pedestrian and banal as those of the life insurance salesman who tries to sell them a plan or the real estate tout with a pile of old brochures.

Powers's priests, otherworldly or foreign as they might be in the popular imagination, are concerned with what "the Arch downtown" thinks of them as much as any working stiff thinks of his or her boss.

They even talk of the church in secular analogies, musing that the Catholic Church is the largest corporation in the world, with branch offices in every town. In *Morte D'Urban*, the title character notes that the Catholic Church is "rated second only to Standard Oil in efficiency," rather more an American goal than a gospel mandate.

"There are no unspeakable sins" in Powers's stories of priests, wrote one reviewer, "just sloth, cruelty, ambition, and pride." His characters "convey authenticity without paroxysm. They inhabit a world embraced by a merciful God and made holy by the Incarnation. Powers offers humor with hope." One gets the sense that while Powers (a daily Massgoer) loved the church immensely, he also saw the artistic value of it—in all its brokenness as well as its beauty—as a background for fiction that traced the vanities and frailties of humankind. In 1964, he said of the institutional church, "there's nothing bigger, cruder, more vulgar in the world."

In many stories, he uses the sometimes-narrow confines of priestly life to show the power of a humbling (humiliating?) moment or two to bring a would-be Icarus back down to earth. Along the way, he always tells a rollicking good tale, full of sly humor and apt observations of the human condition. As a young seminarian in *Wheat That Springeth Green*, Joe Hackett, asks in all sincerity, "How can we make holiness as appealing as sex?" As a world-weary pastor later, he drives past the first liquor store on the road because the proprietors are Catholic; it would be unseemly for a priest to be returning so many empties. Then he passes by the second because the proprietors are Protestant, and that would be worse. Well, *duh*.

Born in 1917 in Jacksonville, Illinois, J. F. Powers studied at Northwestern University in Chicago but never earned a degree. He was one of only a few dozen conscientious objectors in the United States to the Second World War (Gordon Zahn was another) when the concept was not recognized by the U.S. Army. After being briefly imprisoned, Powers was allowed to work as a medical orderly for the war effort. He found his first literary success in 1947 (after and amid various careers as an editor, bookshop proprietor, insurance salesman, and more) with *Prince of Darkness and Other Stories*, a beautiful and somewhat timeless collection.

Two other collections and *Morte D'Urban* followed, and he finished his second and final novel, *Wheat That Springeth Green*, twenty-five long years after his first. He and his wife Betty (also a writer) had five children and moved back and forth from Ireland several times, eventually settling down in Collegeville, Minnesota, where he taught writing.

When Powers died in 1999, the great novelist Jon Hassler said in his eulogy that "since the death eleven years ago of his wife, Betty, he seemed like a man adrift, a solitary soul who cared nothing for convention and seemed to care even less for public opinion." Powers himself was always much more otherworldly than the priests of whom he wrote—with some dire consequences, including times of destitution for him and his family. His inability to finish his second novel also weighed on him; his daughter later wrote that he kept every note of inquiry from his publisher on a spindle on his desk, the stack growing higher year by year.

His letters showed that he always had in mind a novel "about a family man—an artist with ambitions" who is driven down in what she calls "a hopeless contest with human needs and material necessity."

Like the priests of his fiction, J. F. Powers found his ambitions frustrated by the mundane details of life. And yet like those same priests, his work transcended those worldly ambitions.

25

JON HASSLER
Collegeville's No-Gimmicks Sage

The sociologist Joseph Fichter once made a bold procla-
mation about American Catholic culture: "The centers
of creativity in American Catholicism seemed to be concen-
trated in a triangle that reached from St. John's to Chicago to
Notre Dame." The St. John's referenced is St. John's Abbey
of Collegeville, Minnesota, the great Benedictine abbey and
the educational and literary institutions that have grown up
around it.

St. John's is known to church historians for its important
role in liturgical reform (starting well before the Second Vatican Council and continuing through it) and for its important influence on church architecture, music, preaching, and
more. Bookworms might also know it for a 1955 alumnus of
St. John's College who spent much of his life on and around
the campus: the novelist Jon Hassler.

If you don't remember Jon Hassler, it may be because he
never much felt the need to stray too far from his roots in the
Upper Midwest, either in his life or his fiction. Born in Min-
neapolis, he became a high school teacher in Minnesota after
graduating from St. John's. In 1960, he earned a master's
degree from the University of North Dakota—with a thesis

on moral decision-making in the novels of Ernest Hemingway—and from 1965 until 1980, he taught at various area colleges, including St. John's, where he became writer in residence in 1980.

When he died in 2008, his obituary in the *New York Times* quoted a review from 1997 by Diana Postlethwaite, a professor of English literature at St. Olaf College in Northfield, Minnesota, of Hassler's 1997 novel *The Dean's List*: "Forget Garrison Keillor and the Coen brothers. Jon Hassler is Minnesota's most engaging cultural export."

Hassler started out writing short stories, using John Cheever as his model, and turned one story into his first novel, *Staggerford*, in 1977. His short stories and novels were straightforward affairs, written simply but eloquently, the language reflecting the no-nonsense and practical lives of his characters. The novelist Richard Russo noted in 1990 that "Mr. Hassler is one of those writers who make storytelling look so easy that the severe guardians of contemporary literature may be suspicious. Part of Jon Hassler's brilliance has always been his ability to achieve the depth of real literature through such sure-handed, no-gimmicks, honest language that the result appears effortless."

Though Hassler himself once told the Associated Press that he liked to write about misfits—"You can't write a novel about somebody who's perfectly happy"—*Staggerford* and many of his other books were at least in part autobiographical. "On the surface it is the story of a burnt-out high school teacher in the small, fictional northern Minnesota town of Staggerford," wrote Ed Block in a 2015 appreciation of Hassler, and "readers will marvel at the picture of a high-school teacher's drudgery and the sheer exuberance of the satire and the humor." Block, who later wrote an intellectual biography,

Jon Hassler—Voice of the Heartland, wrote that by the novel's end, "the reader is left with a sense of grace and mystery despite the tragedy."

Staggerford was followed by a novel every few years for two decades, eleven novels in all. The famous priest-sociologist (and author of novels of a, ahem, racier nature than Hassler's), Andrew Greeley, identified four of Hassler's novels—*Staggerford, North of Hope, A Green Journey,* and *Dear James*—as books that "might have a critical impact on the self-understanding of Catholics of the importance of religious symbols (*sacramenta*) on Catholic life" in a 2008 article in which he described Hassler as "the last Catholic novelist."

"Hassler's work, I suspect, is not well known among Catholics, even Catholics who teach literature, because it is not grim enough," Greeley wrote. "The proper model, the teachers might say for Catholic fiction, is Flannery O'Connor or Léon Bloy. Or, as I say to my friend John Shea, it is a story that is entirely dark until the strike of one bolt of lightning, which briefly and suddenly illuminates the sky and then permits the darkness to return." Hassler, however, located his epiphanies and moments of grace in simpler things, like a reconciliation between lovers or a kindness done by a former teacher to a troubled student. "As the country priest says at the end of George Bernanos's *Diary*, grace is everywhere," Greeley wrote. "It was Jon Hassler's gift that he saw that presence of grace."

Hassler had a sense for the unease experienced by many Catholics during the 1960s, both because of the innovations wrought by the Second Vatican Council and because of rapidly changing social mores. A nun in *Dear James* scandalizes some of the congregation by beginning prayers at a funeral with, "Our Mother who art in heaven," for example, and the

priest-protagonist of *North of Hope* falls in love in middle age
with his childhood sweetheart and contemplates leaving the
priesthood.

Hassler's recurring character of Agatha McGee (the no-
nonsense schoolteacher of his *Staggerford* novels, based in
part on Hassler's own mother) was fairly consistently portrayed as resenting—or ignoring—any changes in the
church after the council. "Hassler said on a number of occasions that Agatha's conservative, pre-Vatican-II Catholicism
expressed a part of himself," Block wrote, "observing that
when Agatha complained about the church's excesses, it
relieved him from having to do so."

In an obituary for Hassler's fellow Collegeville homebody
J. F. Powers in 1999, Hassler captured Powers's pleasant but
brooding mien but also conveyed something of the tight
bonds the Collegeville community had. The two authors ran
into each other in the post office or at the library more than
anywhere else; neither strayed far from either.

In 2008, *America* honored Hassler as its latest recipient
of the Edmund Campion Award, given to a distinguished
person of letters, for his novels that "examined with infinite
compassion the lives of the residents of small-town Minnesota, and typically touched on overtly Catholic themes. . . .
His lapidary writing and wondrous ability to create fully
formed characters—alive physically, mentally, emotionally,
and spiritually—marked all his fiction." Because Hassler
died on March 20 of that year, his widow, Gretchen Hassler,
accepted the award at a ceremony in Collegeville on his
behalf.

The setting would surely have pleased Jon Hassler: why go
all the way to New York when Collegeville is already here?

26

FULTON SHEEN
The OG Televangelist

"What Is to Be Done with the Body of Fulton Sheen?" That remains my favorite headline of all time, one that graced a story I reported for *America* in October 2017 on a legal battle between the Diocese of Peoria and the Archdiocese of New York. At stake were the mortal remains of Archbishop Fulton Sheen, who was born in Peoria (well, not really; he was born in nearby El Paso, Illinois) but who had been buried according to his wishes in New York's St. Patrick's Cathedral (well, not really; he had asked to be buried in a cemetery in nearby Queens). At the time, Archbishop Sheen's cause for sainthood was gaining steam, and both Peoria and New York thought he belonged with them.

The story had everything: a lawyer who had run for governor of New York in 2014 on the Sapient Party ticket; a plaintiff who arrived with an entourage of nuns; a quintessentially New York argument as to why anyone would want to be buried anywhere else but New York; and references to a long Catholic history of, well, settling these disputes by sending a piece of the body here and a piece there until everyone was satisfied.

Peoria won in the end: in 2019, Archbishop Sheen's remains were disinterred from St. Patrick's Cathedral and flown to Peoria. His cause for sainthood has been on hold since, apparently because of questions about Archbishop Sheen's handling of priest sex abusers during his tenure as bishop of Rochester, New York—but his tomb is now in Peoria's cathedral and a nearby museum chronicles his life and works.

Before the term even existed, Archbishop Sheen was the foremost televangelist in the United States. Beginning with his radio show in the 1930s through several television shows that ran into the late 1960s, he attracted an audience of tens of millions (Catholics and non-Catholics alike) who treasured his gift for making sense of complex religious and spiritual material. He also wrote seventy-three books. When he appeared on the cover of *Time* in 1952, the magazine called him "perhaps the most famous preacher in the U.S., certainly America's best-known Roman Catholic priest, and the newest star of U.S. television."

If you're not familiar with his famous television show, *Life Is Worth Living*, the televangelist and his famous chalkboard can still be found on YouTube. (His surname was also taken by another television and movie star who was a fan of that show in the 1950s—Ramón Estevez, better known to us as Martin Sheen.)

Made an auxiliary bishop of New York in 1951, Sheen found himself at odds with Cardinal Francis Spellman of New York at various points, and some biographers have claimed Spellman forced Sheen to surrender his spot as host of *Life Is Worth Living* in 1958. In 1966, Sheen was made bishop of Rochester in upstate New York, but he resigned the position three years later and was made archbishop of Newport, Wales, a titular see. He died on December 9, 1979, at the age of eighty-four, and was interred in the crypt of St. Patrick's Cathedral in New York City, where he remained until 2019.

Sheen's literary output also included articles for various Catholic journals, including an essay headlined "When Stalin Kissed Hitler the Communists Blushed Red," which is 1930s clickbait for sure. In one 1936 essay, he argued that Catholicism was the only effective counter to communism, because "The world is no longer broadminded; it wants intolerance. There are only two kinds from which the world can choose; the intolerance of Communism and the intolerance of Catholicism."

A quarter-century after his death, in 2004, his literary executor, Patricia Kossmann, wrote a tribute to Sheen. She had met Sheen while working as an editor at Doubleday (where she edited his books *From the Angel's Blackboard* and *Simple Truths*), and remained friends with him until his death. Though Sheen was remarkably prolific as an author and speaker—in addition to his books and shows, he also wrote two syndicated weekly newspaper columns—Kossmann noted that "it was perhaps the three-hour-long Good Friday services at St. Patrick's Cathedral and then St. Agnes Church on East 43th Street (renamed Fulton J. Sheen Place after his death) for which he is most fondly remembered by New Yorkers."

"One of the most celebrated Catholic prelates of the 20th century, Fulton Sheen was an intellectual giant and forceful communicator, whose impact on Catholicism and American culture was due largely to his superb and effective use of the media," Kossmann wrote. The onetime postulator of Sheen's cause, the late Andrew Apostoli, C.F.R. (who was ordained a priest by Sheen in 1967), told Kossmann, "No one could speak in such depth of spirituality and have such a profound effect on people of all walks of life and of all ages without being a very holy person. Closeness to God makes one a greater instrument of his grace to others."

Father Apostoli also noted that Sheen's vast TV audience was made up of more non-Catholics than Catholics. "They listened to him because he spoke the truth with sincerity, and they deeply respected him for it. His is a voice that should never be allowed to remain silent," Kossmann concluded.

When Archbishop Sheen died in 1979, one obituary eulogized him thus:

> The secret of Archbishop Sheen's power was his combination of an educated and thinking head with a generous and feeling heart. Like every great figure in Christian history, Fulton Sheen regularly ascribed his gifts and his effectiveness to God. . . . [And] if Archbishop Sheen had not disposed himself to be the instrument of divine action, he would never have become the greatest evangelizer in the history of the Catholic Church in the United States.

27

THEOPHILUS LEWIS

From Harlem to Rome

Among the cultural touchstones of the Harlem Renaissance in the 1920s was a magazine with a small circulation but an outsized influence on African American culture at the time: the *Messenger*. Founded in 1917 by A. Philip Randolph and Chandler Owen and staunchly socialist in its political views, the magazine initially declared that "economics and politics take precedence to music and art," but eventually took on a more literary tone. It also eventually expanded its list of authors to include Black writers from around the United States.

Drama, particularly African American drama, was an early focus of the magazine, in large part because of the efforts of a theater critic and journalist with an unforgettable name: Theophilus Lewis. Born in 1891 in Baltimore, Lewis moved to New York in 1922 after serving in World War I. A longtime employee of the U.S. Postal Service, Lewis began writing book reviews and theater criticism for the *Messenger* not long after his arrival. He held a dim view of much of the dramatic offerings of the time, in part because he deplored the musicals and low-brow comedies that dominated theaters.

An aficionado of small theaters that treated important

social and political issues, Lewis was also critical of the way mainstream directors tended to push African American actors away from sophisticated or challenging roles. Only the development of a national Black theater that employed Black playwrights and actors, he argued, would prevent Black actors from being relegated to vulgar comedies or simplistic musical roles.

The *Messenger* struggled financially throughout its tenure, and writers like Lewis were often unpaid. The magazine also faced harassment from the federal government (including the arrest of its editors on charges they had violated the Espionage Act) because of its criticism of American involvement in World War I. "No intelligent Negro is willing to lay down his life for the United States as it now exists," the editors wrote in July 1918. "Intelligent Negroes have now reached the point where their support of the country is conditional."

The magazine folded in 1928. Lewis, who also briefly had his own magazine, the *Looking Glass*, went on to write book and theater reviews for other African American newspapers, including the *Pittsburgh Courier*. In 1939, he became a Catholic, and over the next several decades contributed regular theater reviews to *America, Catholic World,* and *Commonweal.* While many of his reviews were straightforward theater criticism, he also continued to write on the themes he had pursued at the *Messenger.*

A classic example is a 1946 essay on Lena Horne, who had recently bemoaned the fact that African Americans like herself were often encouraged to be singers and musicians rather than actors. "When Miss Horne was being interviewed she was probably thinking of numerous talented Negro actors who are unknown because the color bar denied them an opportunity to appear on the American stage," Lewis wrote.

"Her remarks are relevant to the current doldrums in the theatre, because full recognition of the Negro actor may be precisely what is needed to reinvigorate our stagnant drama."

A 1961 review of Robert Bolt's *A Man for All Seasons* began with a classic Lewis opening line: "While the Broadway theatre generally is mediocre at best, and too often meretricious or nauseous, it occasionally rises to maturity." He had high praise for the play, which starred Paul Scofield as Sir Thomas More and would be made into a movie a few years later: "By a marvel of dramatic writing, the play is as exciting as if Sir Thomas engaged the king in a duel or fist fight. As a stage production, the drama is magnificent."

Lewis was less enthusiastic about another debut, Arthur Miller's *Death of a Salesman* in 1949: "Since it is practically certain that *Death of a Salesman* will be elected best of the season, its accolade warrants a re-appraisal of its dramatic and social importance. In either department, the play is no better than second class," he wrote. "While some of the author's admirers call the drama a criticism of our national values, it is never quite clear which popular fallacies are the targets of his censure," Lewis continued.

"Are his strictures intended to debunk the myths and vainglory that have elevated salesmanship to the status of a perverted religion, like voodooism or the nudist sect, or is the salesman a symbol of the inadequacy of material success? If the former were his intention, he has done a good job; if the latter, his treatment of the subject is superficial, faltering, and rather dated."

Lewis's output from 1937 through 1961 was prodigious by any measure; he published more than five hundred theater reviews and more than one hundred contributions in other areas, including book reviews, cultural criticism (including promoting small African American newspapers), and spiritual reflections for magazines. He died in 1974.

During the years it employed Lewis as its prolific drama critic, *America* adopted a far more aggressive and progressive tone regarding racial justice and social issues, a transformation usually credited to the efforts of John LaFarge, S.J., editor in chief of the magazine from 1944 to 1948 and a longtime associate editor before and after. But to my thinking it was Theophilus Lewis's incisive cultural commentary and consistent promotion of African American cultural enterprises in its pages that made the difference.

28

MOIRA WALSH
Sage of the Silver Screen

On June 14, 1947, Moira Walsh wrote her first article for *America,* the beginning of a weekly column of movie reviews, all possessed from Day One of an invincible authorial voice and an encyclopedic knowledge of film history. Her final article was a review of three films: *Murder on the Orient Express*, starring Albert Finney and directed by Sidney Lumet; *A Little Prince*, directed by Stanley Donen; and *Amarcord*, directed by Federico Fellini. It appeared on December 21, 1974—twenty-seven years after her first byline.

In between were 750 columns featuring reviews of more than 1,500 films. Moira Walsh also found time to review movies for the Legion of Decency, a Catholic group dedicated to identifying objectionable content in movies and ranking films for their suitability. Note that Walsh was writing in an era without streaming video or online media; further, there were no screeners or advance copies of films. Her literary output required her to go to the movie theater several times a week. One can only imagine the amount of *Sitzfleisch* that required—and the number of truly terrible films she sat through.

Of the sharp tone Walsh evinced from her first review

throughout the years, perhaps her finest shot was the devastating takedown of the 1956 movie *The Girl Can't Help It*, starring Jayne Mansfield, whose buxom appearance had been a source of constant comment from other reviewers at the time. Walsh began with a blowtorch:

> What the girl can't help is, presumably, that she is shaped like a pouter pigeon or, more accurately, like a grotesque hybrid plant in which one particular feature has been encouraged at the expense of the whole. In any case, the truth of the title statement is open to serious question. Open to even more serious question is the propriety of the studio exploiting Miss Mansfield and similar blonde phenomena in a manner having nothing to do with any talent they may or may not possess.

Alongside Walsh's acid take on Jayne Mansfield's appeal is a remonstration of the studio exploiting her, a trope that would appear with some regularity in Walsh's columns. She had no time for salacious films or ribald content, but at the same time she directed her ire at the forces behind the silver screen rather than those trying to make a living in an industry determined to use sex to sell.

Walsh had a similar objection to *Bye Bye Birdie* in 1963, a film adaptation of a popular satirical play, in which Jesse Pearson played teen idol Conrad Birdie and whose Elvis-like pelvic gyrations made for titillating cinema. The movie, she noted, belonged to a genre that was "skillfully tailored to appeal to teen-agers and giving tacit, uncritical approval to contemporary teen-age mores." Walsh, however, recognized that beyond the mores, the audience, and the actors, the real villain was director George Sidney, who chose to film

Pearson "in a deliberately suggestive fashion." A "bad camera angle can belie a professed good intention," she wrote, so that "the story tells us one thing while the camera says something entirely different."

Walsh herself was as reserved on personal detail in her writing as she was free on opinions regarding cinema, and seems to have enjoyed being something of an enigma. A 1965 article in the *Font*, the student newspaper of Fontbonne College in St. Louis, Missouri, reported that Walsh had visited the campus in early November of that year, titling the story, "Moira Walsh Baffles Students."

When I lamented my inability to track down any biographical information on her in 2023, I received a lovely note from one of her nieces:

> My Aunt Moira (Walsh) would certainly have enjoyed reading your article about her work. My Dad's sister, Moira, was respected, revered, and adored by my seven brothers and sisters and I. Her wit and sense of humor entertained our every family gathering. She was the smartest woman we knew! She died on January 13, 1996, and we continue to miss her.

She is described in various other newspapers of the time as an esteemed critic, and occasionally her name appears without modifier, as if true cinéastes knew her by name alone. In a 2021 article in *American Catholic Studies*, church historian Paul G. Monson called Walsh "one of the most respected Catholic film critics of the 1960s."

Walsh was not always a harsh critic; a survey of her reviews shows she appreciated movies on their own merits and as part of a distinct art form—which might explain how she sat through so many of them. *Pillow Talk*, for example, an inch-deep 1959 movie starring Rock Hudson and Doris Day, earned Walsh's praise as "a romantic farce that is a good deal funnier and more inventive than most comedies." While she didn't approve of the romantic weekend getaway featured in the movie, she did note that the movie "does try to maintain the proper balance between reality and unreality and to focus its jokes so that they are poking fun at human frailties, not approving of them."

In her 1966 review of the film adaptation of *A Man for All Seasons*, she noted a tension that appeared time and again in her reviews over the years: movies were supposed to entertain, but movies should also edify and educate the viewer. How to thread the needle between movies that work as entertainment and movies that instruct one in the moral life? "I agree that a film can accomplish nothing unless it first entertains," she wrote. "I would further suggest that, in practice, few films that entertain do, in fact, elevate, though this is an area about which we know shockingly little and are further handicapped by thinking we know a lot of things that 'ain't so.'"

You might imagine, then, that Bernardo Bertolucci's X-rated *Last Tango in Paris* would not strike Walsh's fancy. But her 1973 review showed once again that Walsh wasn't just the scowling censor from the Legion of Decency. Yes, the movie was sexually explicit in a way that would have been forbidden just a few years before—but maybe, Walsh suggested, it was better that way:

> Though the millennium has not arrived, I also suspect that this is a comparatively healthy development. That judgment is based, not on approval of today's excesses, but on the conviction that the massive *covert*

traffic in pornography and prostitution of the Victorian era, and even the informal stag-movie rituals of more recent years, contributed to the continuing, unexamined degradation of, and acceptance of male myths about, women.

To be sure, Walsh didn't like the film: "If this is a breakthrough," she wrote, "I'll eat my mid-Victorian bonnet." Nevertheless, she found that "Bertolucci, like so many of the young breed of filmmakers, is so proficient with the tools of his trade that the virtuosity of his pacing and visual composition frequently obscures the immaturity and silliness of his vision."

29

Evelyn Waugh
Acid-Tongued Wayfarer

Two decades of working in Catholic media have convinced me that there are certain figures whose every utterance or act requires coverage, reflection, and possibly dissection. Whether it's Bruce Springsteen, Dorothy Day, Flannery O'Connor, or Thomas Merton, I am convinced that progressive Catholics can't go more than a fortnight without mentioning at least one of them. Forgive me if I never, ever want to read another story about Bruce Springsteen's Catholic imagination.

However, not until recently did I discover our forebears were no different; but their Bruce Springsteen was Evelyn Waugh. From the first mentions in the early 1930s of "the brilliant young novelist" who had become Catholic the year before up until, well, a paragraph ago, the guy has never been far from the minds of Catholic readers, writers, and editors.

In recent years, authors like Jon Sweeney, Jessica Hooten Wilson, David Leigh, and Joshua Hren, among many others, have offered their takes on the great novelist and satirist. A more dated but still pertinent article appeared in *America* on April 10, 1993, titled "Portrait of the Artist as a Christian Wayfarer." Written by John W. Donohue, S.J., an associate editor of the magazine from 1972 until 2007 (yes, you read those dates right), the article mentioned Waugh's short stories, travelogues, essays, and biographies, but focused largely on his fourteen novels.

"Taken together," Donohue wrote, "these novels amount to a work of such perfection that Graham Greene, in a memorial notice after Waugh's death, called him 'the greatest novelist of my generation.'"

The 1930s; the 1990s; the 2020s: how can the same author be lauded across so many generations? Especially one who never won any bonus points for being nice, or even decent? As Joshua Hren has noted, Waugh "had a proclivity toward cruelty," to put it mildly. When asked by his friend Nancy Mitford how he could be so terrible toward others while also professing to be a Christian, Waugh replied that "were he not a Christian he would be even more horrible . . . and anyway would have committed suicide years ago."

Waugh, born in 1903, arrived on the English literary scene at the age of twenty-five with his debut novel (after two nonfiction efforts), the satirical *Rise and Fall*, and became a commercial success with his second effort, *Vile Bodies* (1930). He had been educated at Oxford, though according to Waugh himself, his main interests at the time were carousing and naps. "I do no work here," Donohue quotes Waugh in a letter to a friend, "and never go to Chapel." In 1928, he was married to a woman also named Evelyn, leading friends to call them "Evelyn and She-velyn." The marriage collapsed within a year, as She-velyn began a romance with one of Waugh's friends, and the marriage was annulled years later.

In 1930, Waugh became a Roman Catholic, writing to his friend (and longtime interlocutor) Martin D'Arcy, S.J., that he had realized "the Roman Catholic Church is the only genuine form of Christianity." Waugh was a big enough name after *Vile Bodies* was published that his decision made headlines in the London papers. He later described his reception into the Catholic Church as "like stepping across the chimney piece out of a Looking-Glass world, where everything is an absurd caricature, into the real world God made; and then begins the delicious process of exploring it limitlessly."

His novels from then on kept their satirical edge (so did Waugh), but also became more religious in theme; Waugh argued that his fellow Modernist fiction writers sought "to represent the whole human mind and soul and yet omit its determining character—that of being God's creature." He remarried in 1937, to Laura Herbert (she was a cousin of She-velyn; *British aristocrats, amirite?*), and they had seven children, one of whom died in infancy.

After service in the Second World War, Waugh settled into the life of a full-time writer. Though he traveled extensively, he never learned to drive and refused to use the telephone. His signature novel was *Brideshead Revisited*, whose commercial and critical success made Waugh financially secure and all the more famous, but he also gained a certain fame (and notoriety) for several visits to the United States and the scathing reports he delivered after. He had a special antipathy toward "the bloody Yanks," whom he considered "barbaric, vulgar, and bereft of tradition."

In *The Loved One*, Waugh's on-the-nose sendup of Southern California's absurd funeral customs, the protagonist finds himself "exiled in the barbarous regions of the world." The British protagonist finds one positive trait among Americans: they "don't expect you to listen." Even better, "Nothing they say is designed to be heard."

That anti-American streak was tempered over time;

Waugh eventually wrote more positive pieces about the U.S. church and donated the profits from the paperback version of *The Loved One* to the U.S. bishops. "We also forget how he mentored a young Thomas Merton in the late 1940s as the sage editor for the British editions of two of the young Trappist's books, including *The Seven Storey Mountain*, which was retitled *Elected Silence* in England," Jon Sweeney wrote in 2013. Waugh even wrote in a letter to a friend at the time: "It seems to me likely that American monasticism may help save the world."

In 2017, in his review of Philip Eade's biography of Waugh, David Leigh noted that Waugh's later years were troubled by depression and family strife. (Waugh once said, "I am very contentedly married. I have numerous children whom I see once a day for 10, I hope, awe-inspiring minutes.") A heavy drinker, Waugh had also become dependent on sedatives to sleep. During a 1954 trip to Ceylon, he suffered what appeared to be a nervous breakdown (likely brought on by his drug use), an experience later fictionalized in the novel *The Ordeal of Gilbert Pinfold*.

Another unhappy development for Waugh was the Second Vatican Council, as he decried the changes the council wrought in the Catholic Church. Before the council was even long underway, Waugh had penned open letters in 1963 to the gathered bishops (published in the *National Review* and the *London Spectator*) lamenting the anticipated renewal in the church; he was particularly appalled by the notion of a "priesthood of the laity" the council promulgated.

His experience of the postconciliar church was also not a happy one. Not long before his death in 1966, he wrote, "I have not yet soaked myself in petrol and gone up in flames, but I now cling to the Faith doggedly without joy."

Waugh died on April 10, 1966, a few hours after Easter Sunday Mass. A decade previous, he had written the following to the poet Elizabeth Sitwell, his goddaughter, on the occasion of her reception into the Catholic Church (and akin to Nancy Milford's remark): "I always think to myself, 'I know I am awful. But how much more awful I should be without the Faith.' One of the joys of Catholic life is to recognize the little sparks of good everywhere, as well as the fire of the saints."

30

THICH NHAT HANH
Peace and Mindfulness

After Thich Nhat Hanh died at the age of ninety-five on January 22, 2022, many obituary writers turned to his 1965 book, *Vietnam: Lotus in a Sea of Fire*, for quotes and for an assessment of the "engaged Buddhism" the Zen Buddhist monk had taught and promoted for many years. But that book was only one of many written by the prolific author, peace activist, poet, and teacher. A passage from his 1975 book, *The Miracle of Mindfulness*, perhaps better captures the sense of wonder behind his teaching and ministry:

> Every day, we are engaged in a miracle which we don't even recognize: a blue sky, white clouds, green leaves, the black, curious eyes of a child, our own two eyes. All is a miracle.

Nhat Hanh's promotion of engaged Buddhism—the application of Buddhist principles to political and social issues—revealed his understanding of Buddhism as a way of nonviolence, mindfulness, and compassion. Well into his eighties, he continued to find eager audiences for his teachings; his 2012 book, *The Art of Mindfulness*, sold over two hundred thousand copies in the United States alone. He also inspired and collaborated with many leading figures in the U.S. antiwar movement, including Daniel Berrigan, S.J., and Thomas Merton.

Born on October 11, 1926, in Hue, Vietnam, Nhat Hanh expressed a desire to become a Buddhist monk from an early age, officially beginning his training at a Zen monastery at the age of sixteen. Already known by the 1950s as a spiritual teacher, Nhat Hanh came to greater prominence in Vietnam in 1964 when he founded and organized the School of Youth Social Service, which recruited young volunteers to restore villages destroyed by bombings and to build schools and hospitals.

That same year, he published a poem, "Condemnation," that led to accusations from all sides—in the U.S., Vietnam, and elsewhere—of his holding the wrong political sympathies, and some labeled him a Communist sympathizer. "Whoever is listening, be my witness," the poem read in part. "I cannot accept this war. / I never could I never will."

In "Mindful Monks," a 2002 review of *Dialogues with Silence* and *Thomas Merton and Thich Nhat Hanh: Engaged Spirituality in an Age of Globalization*, Richard J. Hauser, S.J., noted that both Nhat Hanh and Thomas Merton "began as monks committed to a cloistered contemplative life, and both gradually found their vocations—leading them to prophetic social involvement."

In 1966 Nhat Hanh visited the United States on a lecture tour, in part to speak to the American people about the war (Nhat Hanh had studied at Princeton Theological Seminary in the early 1960s and was fluent in English). He met with a number of politicians and religious leaders, including Martin Luther King Jr. and Thomas Merton. In May of that year,

Nhat Hanh visited Merton at the Abbey of Gethsemani in Kentucky. In a 2022 tribute to Nhat Hanh, Gregory Hillis relayed how a mutual friend described their encounter:

> The two conversed late into the night. They talked about monastic chant, about meditation in each other's traditions, about monastic formation. And they talked about the Vietnam War.

A number of years later, Nhat Hanh recalled their meeting fondly: "Conversation with him was so easy," he said. "He was open to everything. . . . He wanted to know more and more. He did not talk so much about himself. He was constantly asking questions. And then he would listen." He continued: "I was impressed by his capacity for dialogue."

Nhat Hanh had planned to speak to the monks at Gethsemani, but after Nhat Hanh lost his voice, Merton stood in for him. "The talk was recorded, and it is clear from the tape that Merton was impressed by the Vietnamese monk," Hillis wrote. "Describing Nhat Hanh as 'an extremely simple, humble person,' Merton told his brothers that Nhat Hanh was 'a completely formed monk' with whom he felt in 'complete contact.'"

Writing in *Jubilee* magazine later that year, Merton wrote of Nhat Hanh that "He is more my brother than many who are nearer to me by race and nationality, because he and I see things exactly the same way" regarding the war in Vietnam. "Nhat Hanh may be returning to imprisonment, torture, even death. We cannot let him go back to Saigon to be destroyed while we sit here, cherishing the warm humanitarian glow of good intentions and worthy sentiments about the ongoing war," Merton wrote. "We who have met and heard Nhat Hanh, or who have read about him, must also raise our voices to demand that his life and freedom be respected when he returns to this country."

Nhat Hanh eventually found himself banned from both North and South Vietnam. He moved to a community in southern France that would later become Plum Village, Europe's largest Buddhist monastery. Though he would be much sought after as a speaker and teacher around the world in the decades after the Vietnam War, he would not return to his home country until 2005. In the intervening years most of his books were smuggled in. He became well known around the globe for his teachings on mindfulness and is considered a major influence in bringing the tenets of Buddhism to the West. Among his published works are over one hundred books in English. Over the years, he also led Buddhist spiritual retreats for politicians, economists, and even Silicon Valley techies, including a daylong retreat at Google in 2013. Yes, Google.

Nhat Hanh suffered a stroke in 2014 that affected his speech and movement. He finally moved permanently back to Vietnam in 2018, spending the last years of his life at the Tu Hieu Temple where he had been a novice many years before.

In 1967, Dr. Martin Luther King Jr. had nominated Nhat Hanh for the Nobel Peace Prize (it was ultimately awarded to no one that year). "I do not personally know of anyone more worthy than this gentle monk from Vietnam," he wrote to the Nobel Institute. "His ideas for peace, if applied, would build a monument to ecumenism, to world brotherhood, to humanity."

31

MURIEL SPARK
Flesh on the Human Predicament

While doing some research on John L'Heureux (he's else-where in this volume!), I had the occasion to reread *Picnic in Babylon*, the memoir of his years studying theology when the great poet and fiction writer was still a Jesuit priest. Between the scholars he met and the writers whose work he was devouring, the book contains some delightful name-dropping, including one that surprised L'Heureux himself at the time: Muriel Spark.

Spark was far more prominent as a writer at the time than L'Heureux, who was still a seminarian and had published a single book of poetry. Spark, a Scottish poet-turned-novelist (though she considered novels inferior, "a lazy way of writing poetry"), was at the height of her popularity, particularly for her novels *The Comforters, Memento Mori, The Prime of Miss Jean Brodie, The Girls of Slender Means,* and *The Mandelbaum Gate.* She would author twenty-two novels in all, three of which were nominated for the Booker Prize.

In October of 1965, Spark wrote to L'Heureux, apparently somewhat out of the blue. "Do let me know if you are in New York and can spare the time to come along for a drink," she wrote. "I should enjoy that very much." L'Heureux described himself as "delighted out of my wits. And I *will* meet her sometime." During a visit to New York a few months later, one of L'Heureux's friends canceled a lunch appointment. "I rang up Muriel Spark. She said she would be delighted to have lunch with me."

You'll have to read *Picnic in Babylon* for the rest—suffice it to say that L'Heureux was honored by the attention and somewhat in awe of his lunch companion. Muriel Spark's reputation has not suffered in the decades since—she was made a dame of the British Empire in 1993, and her novels continue to be adapted for stage and screen alike even sixteen years after her death. But the Scottish-born author seems something of a mystery to American readers otherwise; I will admit that though I have taught two of her novels in college courses in the past, I knew little about her personal life until recently.

That life story would make a great novel itself, though it would require more than the usual suspension of disbelief. Spark was never all that forthcoming about her personal affairs: even a 1992 autobiography covering the first four decades of her life, *Curriculum Vitae*, contains as much evasion and obfuscation as revelation. Nevertheless, what biographers have pieced together certainly intrigues.

Born Muriel Camberg in Edinburgh, Scotland, in 1918 to a Jewish father and a Presbyterian mother (though some biographers have argued that both parents may have been Jewish), she moved to what was then Rhodesia at the age of nineteen to marry a thirty-two-year-old math teacher, Sydney Spark. Their marriage was short and unhappy, and Muriel Spark and their son returned to Great Britain. During the Second World War, she worked for British intelligence writing fake news—*fake news!*—for propaganda radio broadcasts.

After the war, Spark began publishing poetry and worked for a time as the editor of the *Poetry Review*; she also collaborated with the journalist Derek Stanford on literary appreciations of Mary Shelley, Emily Brontë, and John Masefield, as well as an edition of the letters of Cardinal John Henry Newman. A romantic affair with an unhappy ending between her and Stanford soured her on the collaboration, though she retained a great interest in Newman, particularly for his literary and poetic sensibilities.

Like her former husband, Sydney, Spark did not always enjoy good mental health. In the throes of a painful addiction to Dexedrine (sold over the counter for weight loss at the time) in the years following, she became convinced that T. S. Eliot was sending her messages in code. During her painful withdrawal from the drug, she suffered from depression. Among the friends and fellow writers who supported her was Graham Greene, who, according to Anne M. Begley, "sent her a small monthly allowance accompanied by a few bottles of red wine to alleviate the sting of charity."

In 1954, Spark became a Roman Catholic with the public support of Greene and Evelyn Waugh, having been baptized in the Church of England just a year before. Novels began appearing in rapid succession, each more inventive than the last.

Her first, *The Comforters* (1957), is a novel about writing a novel; the protagonist hears a typewriter and a narrator in her own head all day long. In *Loitering with Intent*, the protagonist discovers the opposite: everything she writes becomes reality. Perhaps her most famous creations are *The Prime of Miss Jean Brodie* and *Memento Mori*: in the latter, one character after another receives a cryptic phone call stating the famous title phrase: "Remember, you must die."

"Spark's readers are taken on satiric jaunts through various cities, times and places, bringing them face to face, mind to mind, with life's odd, harrowing, real perplexities," wrote Patricia Kossmann in 2001. "With a sharp observational eye (no doubt honed from extensive worldwide travels), she is able to put flesh—eerily familiar flesh at times—on the human predicament and its attendant conflicts. It's all there: good versus evil, honor versus duplicity, self-aggrandizement versus self-pity. And she can be wickedly funny in the process."

In 1955, the editorial board of the Catholic Book Club instituted the Campion Award to honor distinguished Anglo-American writers; recipients over the years have included Jacques Maritain, Frank Sheed and Maisie Ward, T. S. Eliot, Karl Rahner, Raymond Brown, Robert Giroux, Avery Dulles, Annie Dillard, Chinua Achebe, John Updike, and Daniel Berrigan, among many others. In 2001, the recipient of the Campion Award was Muriel Spark.

When the editors of *America* announced the award, literary editor Patricia Kossmann wasn't sure what the response would be: Spark was an octogenarian at the time and had been living in Tuscany for many years. Estranged from her only son and intensely private about her personal life, she was a bit of an unknown. No need to worry. "When informed of our decision, her response was swift and gracious," Kossmann wrote, "even a bit surprising. She wrote: 'I accept this honour with special pleasure in that I have been a devoted admirer of Edmund Campion, both as martyr and writer, for many years. I possess a reliquary containing a treasured relic of Father Campion, and of course I know Evelyn Waugh's fine work on the saint.'"

Spark was, wrote Robert E. Hosmer Jr. in a 2018 appreciation, "always in complete control of both character and plot," in her fiction and in her life. She received the Campion Award in absentia, declining the customary formal reception and dinner in New York City. She died five years later in Florence, Italy, and is buried in Tuscany.

Her simple gravestone, reading "Muriel Spark, Poeta, 1918–2006," stands in contrast to the many encomiums given on her behalf in her final years, including one from the *Sunday Telegraph* that surely raised an eyebrow or two among her fellow Scots: "Britain's greatest living novelist."

32

SALMAN RUSHDIE
The End of the Age of Heroes

The attack on Salman Rushdie on August 12, 2022, in Chautauqua, New York, was a stark reminder of how quickly our illusions of safety and order can be shattered. How does a book reading turn into an attempted murder? It was also a reminder that the author has lived under a death sentence for—count 'em—thirty-five years. His condemnation to death by the ruler of Iran had become a sometimes-remembered question of historical intolerance and an interesting footnote in the relationship between Islam and the West. But while Rushdie survived the assault, it is clear the threat against him has never really gone away.

Rushdie's novel *The Satanic Verses* was published in 1988. The next year, Iran's Ayatollah Khomeini issued a fatwa against Rushdie, declaring that he, "along with all the editors and publishers aware of its contents, are condemned to death" for what was seen as the book's blasphemy against Allah and ridicule of Islam (Khomeini, according to his own son, never actually read the book). At the time, Rushdie and the British government took the threat quite seriously, in part because the government of Iran backed it up with a

$6 million bounty on Rushdie's head. The British government severed diplomatic relations with Iran over the incident.

The controversy of course made *The Satanic Verses* a runaway bestseller—"the best known and least read book of the twentieth century," wrote one reporter—but Rushdie spent nine long years in hiding before resuming a moderately normal life. Over the past two decades he has returned to publishing novels regularly (eight since *The Satanic Verses*), along with many other works, including a memoir of his experience of living under the fatwa, 2012's *Joseph Anton* (his alias during those years), and a 2024 memoir about the attack, *Knife*.

The Satanic Verses "appears destined to be one of the most controversial and certainly the most publicized novels in history," wrote the Rev. Elias D. Mallon in April 1989, a month after the fatwa was announced. "The controversy surrounding the novel is a paradigm of the difficulties that have existed over the centuries between Islam and the West. What was once a conflict between 'Christendom' and Islam has now shifted to a conflict between Islam and pluralistic democracies." A scholar engaged in Christian–Muslim dialogue, Father Mallon found it "a classic example of two world views not understanding each other—and doing it with passion and conviction."

Part of the blame, Mallon wrote, could be laid at the feet of well-meaning attempts to paper over differences between the two faiths in pursuit of an endless string of areas of agreement. It comes as a rough shock when "Christians discover that Muslims do not share many of the values of the pluralistic West and Muslims discover that Western religious sensitivities are quite different from those of Islam." Nor should Westerners, he warned, be all that quick to see Rushdie as a babe in the woods in the controversy: "He was born a Muslim and grew up familiar with Islam. Islam's intense sensitivity toward its central personages and symbols cannot have been something of which Rushdie was unaware," Mallon wrote. "None of this justifies death threats, book burnings, and calls for censorship. It does, however, caution against looking upon Rushdie as a totally innocent victim, ignorant of the storm that he was about to unleash."

Mallon suggested that the controversy offered a teachable lesson for everyone. For Christians, it could be a challenge to understand Islam and Muslims better: "The fact that Christians are almost totally unfamiliar with so many of the central symbols and most important personalities of Islam is a sign that there is need for education." For Muslims, it could be a challenge to recognize that "Westerners, who are as profoundly committed to their faith as are Muslims, experience their faith as most secure and most free to practice its beliefs in a society where pluralism is strictly safeguarded" and most expressions of speech are uncensored.

It has been more than three decades since the fatwa was issued, and our political and cultural categories have changed dramatically since 1989. "The Anglo-American world did not yet see militant Islam as its primary enemy. Our bête noire in those days was the dreaded, though crumbling, 'evil empire'—the Soviet Union," I wrote in 2009. The United States had some strange bedfellows at the time, too: "Among our unofficial allies in those days were Saddam Hussein, Iran's implacable enemy, and Osama bin Laden, who was waging jihad against Soviet aggression in Afghanistan with American military aid."

Rushdie is now a resident of New York City, and his 2019 novel, *Quichotte,* is a *Don Quixote*–inspired tale of an aging Indian American traveling across the United States in search of his own Dulcinea. It's not Rushdie's first novel set in the United States; *Grimus*, published in 1975, followed the exploits of an Indigenous person in Arizona who achieves immortality (what can I say, magical realism was a hell of a tester).

In 2017, he published *The Golden House*. According to reviewer Randy Boyagoda, the novel featured "two of the defining concerns of Rushdie's career—his interest (often but not always polemical) in the abiding powers of belief and religion in the modern era, and his interest (often but not always affectionate) in the oversized influence and tumultuous nature of the United States." In his Gatsby-esque novel about the contemporary United States, Rushdie focuses on the personal (in the individual lives of his characters) and the political (in his treatment of the rise of Donald Trump) while keeping his sharp wit.

President Trump "was, after all, a scary clown," Rushdie writes, both because it was so hard to take him seriously and yet impossible to deny his political success: "America had left reality behind and entered the comic-book universe."

Rushdie is at his best, Boyagoda observes, when he is "drawing us toward higher concerns, as when he balances the novel's early celebrations of the self-invention made possible by coming to America with more wistful reflections about the irreducible continuities of our lives."

Ours "is not an age of heroes," says Rushdie in *The Golden House*. Instead, Boyagoda writes, "it is an age of division and violence, one in which the question of the value of human life itself emerges as the question that matters most, both in national life and family life."

33

Shusaku Endo
"Christ Broken and Scorned"

"Hatred can always change to love. When one can say to God, 'I hate you,' it is like saying, 'My God, my God, why have you forsaken me?' With these words authentic prayer begins."

These words might seem counterintuitive to many believers, even blasphemous. How can a rejection of God lead to love of God? Anyone who has read Shusaku Endo's novel *Silence* (or seen Martin Scorsese's 2016 film adaptation) might recognize the sentiment expressed in the quote, however—and with good reason: they are Endo's own words, spoken to William Johnston, S.J., in 1994.

Endo, described on occasion as "the Japanese Graham Greene," is also routinely called the greatest Japanese Catholic novelist (an appellation of which he did not approve) because of his many novels with deeply Catholic themes—all set in a culture which he himself described as deeply alien to Christianity in most respects.

Shusaku Endo was born in Tokyo in 1923 and spent his early years in Manchuria. His parents divorced when he was ten, and he went to live with an aunt in Kobe who had converted to Catholicism (his mother would also later convert). Endo himself was baptized a Catholic in 1934 after a brief period of catechesis, a process a biographer later quoted him as saying was akin to "being outfitted in an ill-fitting suit of Western clothes." During literature studies at Keio University in Japan, he became interested in the works of French novelists like François Mauriac and George Bernanos, and in 1950 he moved to France to study French Catholic writers.

After a bout with tuberculosis forced him to return to Japan, he embarked on a remarkably prolific career: His first novel, published in English as *White Man*, won the prestigious Akutagawa Prize for promising new writers in 1955; in the next five years, he released *Yellow Man*, *The Sea and Poison* (winner of Japan's Shincho Literary Award and Mainichi Cultural Award), *Wonderful Fool*, *Stained Glass Elegies*, and *Volcano*. They would be followed almost yearly by other novels, including *Silence*, *Samurai*, and *Scandal*, and collections of short stories, biographies, essays, and plays.

Many of his protagonists are Christian believers who grapple intensely with the challenges of faith, particularly a faith that feels transplanted into a culture that has its own deep spiritual roots and practices, "where Japan is portrayed as a swampland in which everything foreign, including Christianity, is swallowed up or transformed," in the words of Francis Mathy, S.J., in a 1992 essay.

English speakers were largely introduced to Endo's work upon the 1969 publication of *Silence*, a translation of his 1966 novel, *Chinmoku*, by Johnston, an Irish Jesuit in Japan since 1951 who later became an internationally known speaker on the relationship between Christianity and Zen Buddhism, contemplation, and mysticism. Johnston later recalled that many of his Jesuit colleagues in Tokyo and abroad were less than pleased that of all of Endo's works, he chose to translate *Silence*—the story of a Jesuit missionary in Japan who apostasizes. Johnston and Endo met while Johnston was translating the novel, and remained lifelong friends until Endo's death in 1996.

In a 1969 review of *Silence*, William J. Everett noted that it would "surely give the reader a deeper insight into Oriental attitudes toward historical Christianity and will help him understand more fully the difficulties involved in its putting down roots in the 'swamp of Japan.' Incidentally, it will force everyone to reconsider his own ideas of traitors and heroes, or strong and weak Catholics."

The novel has been adapted three separate times for film, the most famous of which was Scorsese's 2016 adaptation, for which James Martin, S.J., consulted as a theological adviser, later interviewing him on his own thoughts on faith, filmmaking, and why *Silence* was so important to him as a personal project. One surprising revelation: as a young man, Scorsese dreamed of becoming a Maryknoll priest.

One cannot read Endo's other works without suspecting that he offers in *Silence* a counterintuitive take on the nature of Christianity that fit with his own experience of life—as a stranger in his own land, afflicted at a young age with illness, often misunderstood. In *Silence,* the Jesuit missionaries arrive self-assured that the triumph of Christianity—a very Western European Christianity—over Japan is all but inevitable; but they die broken, scorned, barren.

As he related in his 1973 *A Life of Jesus*, Endo identified more with the Christ who had been broken and scorned than he ever did with all the soaring cathedrals and theological or philosophical accomplishments of European Christianity. Like Father Rodrigues in *Silence*, Endo found God less in Christianity's strength than in its moments of most profound weakness.

34

GRAHAM GREENE
"Saint or Cynic?"

Fans of Graham Greene may have seen a new addition in 2023 to a long list of books offering personal takes on the famous author: *My Man in Antibes*, a memoir by Michael Mewshaw on the complicated friendship between the two. Greene's greatness and his foibles are both fully on display in the book, which is actually kinder than most about its subject. Chroniclers of Greene's life have not always been. In 2013, the writer and critic Jon Sweeney noted that Greene had unfairly endured "more malevolent biographers than anyone is due." Greene's official and most comprehensive biographer, Norman Sherry, "exhibits on several occasions an only slightly veiled animosity toward his subject," added Sweeney, who took a more nuanced view of Greene's life and work.

Though Greene's first novel had been published a decade earlier in 1929, it was not until his book *Another Mexico* (published outside the United States as *The Lawless Roads*) appeared in 1939 that the Brit first began to attract significant attention on this side of the pond. A year later, *The Labyrinthine Ways* (the original U.S. title of *The Power and the Glory*) came out to mostly positive reviews, though not without some sniping about Greene's racier passages. One reviewer called it "a novel that will provoke much thought and give rise to many arguments. It will offend some, and disgust others, and I doubt that it will be entirely accepted by many."

Indeed, the book drew the attention of the Congregation for the Doctrine of the Faith (now the Dicastery for the Doctrine of the Faith), which in 1953 appointed two consultants, including a cardinal, to study *The Power and the Glory*. Both criticized the book's depiction of sexual immorality, and Greene was summoned to Westminster Cathedral by Cardinal Bernard Griffin, who listed changes the Vatican thought should be made to the book. Greene declined. In a letter to Greene, his friend (and sometime frenemy) Evelyn Waugh suggested the following course of action: "They have taken 14 years to write their first letter. You should take 14 years to answer it."

Regardless of the inquisitorial opinions of the Holy Office, *The Power and the Glory* (inspired both by *The Lawless Roads* and by the life of Blessed Miguel Pro, S.J., a Mexican martyr) survived to become a classic, despite an initial publishing run of 3,500 books. I first read this curious tale of an outlawed "whiskey priest" who stubbornly refuses to surrender to his political and religious enemies, even unto death, when I was a high school student, at first somewhat unwillingly. The title sounded suspiciously like a catechetical text. But ever since I've been hooked on Greene. I even later read *Monsignor Quixote*, and let's be honest, that book is an acquired taste.

The Power and the Glory was preceded by nine novels and travelogues, including *Brighton Rock*; in the six decades that followed, twenty-two more books—novels, short story collections, and nonfiction works—established Greene as one of the premier English-language writers of the twentieth century. Novels like *The Heart of the Matter, A Burnt-Out Case,* and *The End of the Affair* joined *The Power and the Glory* and *Brighton Rock* as Greene's "Catholic novels," while works like *The Quiet American, The Third Man,* and *Our Man in Havana* made him an exemplar of literarily inclined authors of espionage novels.

In 1948, the author and critic Richard McLaughlin published a lengthy profile, "Graham Greene: Saint or Cynic?" in which the author related an evening spent with Greene discussing literature. "I am firmly convinced that Graham Greene is no ordinary novelist," he wrote. "Not only is he one of our finest craftsmen writing today, but he is so preoccupied with man's inner struggle to save his soul that he is comparable only to our greatest literary masters. His moral fervor, his peculiar concern with man as beset by evil and yearning to reach God through a maze of despair and anguish pervades his writing; but what is even more awesome is to find it so evident in the man's mien and conversation."

Greene was born in 1904 in Hertfordshire, England, to Charles Henry Greene and Marion Raymond Greene, who were themselves first cousins and part of a distinguished British family. He attended Oxford University, where he first encountered Evelyn Waugh (who later wrote that Greene "shared in none of our revelry"), and was briefly affiliated with the Communist Party. After graduation in 1925, he met Vivien Dayrell-Browning. Greene, an agnostic to that point, converted to Catholicism in 1926, and the two were married a year later.

He wrote book and film reviews for many years as a side hustle. (Many of his works have been made into movies as well.) A review of child star Shirley Temple's movie *Wee Willie*

Winkie didn't end well for Greene, and resulted in him briefly leaving the country; he was sued (and lost) for referring to Ms. Temple's "dimpled depravity" and "dubious coquetry."

Greene always wrote by hand, and typically only five hundred words a day, usually in the morning. He traveled far and often and was recognized as a cultural and political commentator as much as a novelist in his prime.

Greene's life and marriage were both affected deeply by his manic depression. He also had a rather complicated relationship with his Catholic faith. He described himself at one point as a "Catholic agnostic," and stopped practicing in the 1950s after he separated from his wife (though they remained legally married until his death). Greene returned to the sacraments in his old age. "I had to find a religion," he once wrote, "to measure my evil against." Like many of his characters, Greene seemed always to be holding up the church as a bulwark of grace and sanity in a world of vice and squalor— including in his personal life. (Look it up somewhere else; I'm not Walter Winchell.)

A strong critic of American foreign policy in the Caribbean, Latin America, and Southeast Asia, he at one point championed Fidel Castro—rather a departure from the sharp criticism of Mexico's secular leftist government to be found in *The Power and the Glory*.

Greene died in 1991 of leukemia and is buried in Courseaux, Switzerland. George Hunt, S.J., commented in 1989 that Greene's novels, along with those of Waugh and George Bernanos, once "filled the personal literary shelves of every self-respecting Catholic intellectual." It has been commonplace since his death (and even during his life) to crown authors "the next Graham Greene," including Shusaku Endo and John Irving, though commentators should remember a classic moment in English literature: In 1949, a British magazine asked readers to submit parodies of Greene's writing style. Greene entered the contest himself under a pseudonym—and won second place.

Not even Graham Greene was the next Graham Greene.

Upon Greene's death, Joseph Feeney, S.J., noted that Greene was one of the hardest novelists to explain to students because he "concealed his art." Feeney compared him to "the Harlem Globetrotters, Beverly Sills or Penn and Teller. I want to let Greene's simplicity shine amid the self-flaunting style of Joyce, Woolf, and Fowles. I enjoy the others' words and wordplay, but I also prize Greene for being so minimal, so focused on story and person, that he refuses the distraction of beautiful words. He is an ascetic of art. His novels are people, his style a mere means."

"With Graham Greene's death," Feeney continued, "we lose a supreme stylist and a master novelist. We also lose a self-styled 'bit of grit' in the Catholic machine. But as this great God-questioner passes to God, he leaves behind his questioning mind in his questioning works."

35

JOHN L'HEUREUX
A Poet's Prayer

A consequence of being a fan of mostly dead authors is that one rarely gets the chance to meet one's heroes in person or through correspondence. Among the more cherished exceptions to this hard truth is a short email exchange I had in 2018 with John L'Heureux, the prolific novelist, short story writer, and poet, who died in April 2019 in Palo Alto, California, at the age of eighty-four. Best known for his novels (including *The Shrine at Altamira, The Handmaid of Desire,* and *The Medici Boy,* among many others) and short stories that regularly appeared in the *New Yorker* and the *Atlantic Monthly,* L'Heureux was a professor of English at Stanford University for thirty-six years and directed the Stanford Writing Program for eleven. His former students are among the nation's leading novelists, poets, and literary critics.

He was also for a time a Jesuit priest, though one with a quixotic history. He entered the Society of Jesus in 1954 ("I was the last generation whose classes were taught in Latin," he once wrote) and quickly earned a reputation for his literary talent—one not always appreciated by his superiors. He told me over email that on his first day of teaching high school as a Jesuit scholastic, the rector of the community informed him, "'We're watching you. We know you write poetry, and publish it, and we've been warned about you.' That was my first-day welcome to Fairfield Prep."

His first book of poetry, *Quick as Dandelions*, was published in 1964 and was quickly followed by two more books of poems and a memoir, *Picnic in Babylon*. (Readers of a certain age may recall L'Heureux's unmatchable description of the famously tall and lanky Avery Dulles, S.J., as "an incredible man: all bony and elongated, made of rake handles and broomsticks and old umbrellas.") After ordination in 1966, L'Heureux briefly studied for a doctorate in English at Harvard, but dropped out to become an editor at the *Atlantic Monthly*. "There I was, on the cover of *Jesuit News*, as a modern Jesuit who worked as an editor all week but took parish calls on the weekend," he told me in 2018. "I was briefly acceptable."

L'Heureux left the Jesuits and the priesthood in 1971. He remained prolific as a writer, though one journal in particular seemed not to care for his work. "When, having left the Jesuits, I began bringing out a novel each year, I seem to recall *America* was there to let its readers know that my work was disappointing," he told me. But his memories of his time in the Jesuits, he told me, were mostly fond ones. "There are also the great men I lived with, including the astro-physicist Provincial who saw me out," he recalled, "and the quiet saints I lived with [for] 17 years."

Tobias Wolff, who had studied under L'Heureux at Stanford, reflected on his former teacher in an adaptation of an introduction he wrote to *Conversations with John L'Heureux*, by Dikran Karagueuzian, in *America* a week after L'Heureux's death. "In reading his work, one can see, feel, the demands he makes on himself for exactitude, essence, emotional honesty, aesthetic freshness, digging deep for the truths of our thoughts and desires, and presenting his findings without flinching," Wolff wrote, "even—no, especially—when they challenge our self-conceptions and certainties, and trouble the heart."

"When you read a novel like *An Honorable Profession* or *The Shrine at Altamira*, a short story like 'The Anatomy of Bliss' or 'Roman Ordinary,' you can't help wishing you could sit down with the writer, ask him how he came to write such a work, how he came to write at all," Wolff wrote. "What were the paths that led him to this life, what surprises did he encounter along the way, what encouragements, what impediments and distractions, disappointments and joys? What has he learned about the art he has practiced so well and for so long, and what has he learned from it?"

One of L'Heureux's early publications had been somewhat lost to history: an experimental eucharistic prayer. How it came about is an odd story, and one that requires some understanding of U.S. Catholic culture in the 1960s.

After the bishops at the Second Vatican Council approved the liturgical constitution "Sacrosanctum Concilium," theologians and liturgists in various linguistic groups around the world began to seek out how best to address the concession allowing for use of the vernacular at Mass. Europeans led the way, but English-speaking Americans were no slackers. A 1969 book edited by Robert F. Hoey, S.J., *The Experimental Liturgy Book*, lists thirty-six new eucharistic prayers among its hundreds of new options for an English-language liturgy.

In 1967, the Vatican gave the bishops of the United States permission to formulate new canons for the Mass in the vernacular. In response, *America* associate editor C. J. McNaspy,

S.J. (you can find that colorful character elsewhere in this volume), asked two Jesuit writers to contribute eucharistic prayers to the conversation. Rather than stolid word-for-word translations of the Latin text, McNaspy and friends were looking for "theologians with a gift of words, and poets who know liturgical theology." They found two in Donald Gelpi, S.J., and John L'Heureux, S.J., the latter ordained only a year, and both published in *America*'s May 27, 1967, issue.

L'Heureux's prayer would be recognizable to us today, though with certain inflections that hint both at his own theology and of the *mise en scène* in which he lived. (That continuity wasn't always true; things got a little squirrelly at times in the late 1960s, liturgically speaking.) In his eucharistic canon, the emphasis on sin and atonement is toned down, with L'Heureux preferring phrasing like, "You have chosen us to be your children, you have called us to a life of joy and love; you have given us your beloved Son." Jesus, in L'Heureux's conception, comes not to judge the living and the dead, but "to do justice to the living and the dead on the day you shall appoint."

Later, his prayer asks that "before the eyes of all men we may live your gospel and be the sacrament of Christ's presence, that we may support one another in love, that our hearts may be open to the poor, the sick, the unwanted, to all who are in need. We pray that thus we may truly be the Church of Jesus Christ, serving one another out of love for you."

It is a simple, unadorned prayer, lacking the baroque prose and Cranmer-influenced phrasing of what was to come in the 1969 Latin Missal. But it is also one reflective of an intense engagement with the joys and struggles of the world. A poet's prayer, from the heart.

36

SALLY ROONEY
A Hemingway Simplicity

I have a lot of opinions about who is the greatest Catholic novelist in the English language, and only most of them end with me shouting "J. F. Powers." I have read convincing arguments for many other authors who hail from either side of the pond, and the Australians, New Zealanders, and Canadians have their own candidates as well. And let's not even get started with those like Nabokov and others who wrote great novels in English even though it wasn't their native tongue. But who is the greatest Catholic novelist in the English language *today*?

That question, too, has been asked every few years since the glory days of the early 1960s, when Powers won the 1962 National Book Award for *Morte D'Urban*, Edwin O'Connor won the 1962 Pulitzer Prize for Fiction for *The Edge of Sadness*, and Walker Percy won the 1963 National Book Award for *The Moviegoer*. Who in recent decades has joined those ranks as a great Catholic novelist? Mary Gordon? Ron Hansen? Alice McDermott? Jon Hassler? Toni Morrison?

If the millennials and Gen Z kids are to be believed (this is known grammatically as an "unreal conditional"), there is a new challenger to the throne: Sally Rooney.

I know, I know: You can't wait for the latest Chosen One to appear drinking a White Claw or pretending to watch football with Travis Kelce's girlfriend. And Muriel Spark never ate avocado toast. But Rooney's fans are serious about her place in the literary pantheon. "If the goal of art from the Catholic perspective is to reveal beauty, truth, and light—to point in the direction of God," wrote Ciaran Freeman in a 2021 review of *Beautiful World, Where Are You*, "then Sally Rooney is my generation's great Catholic writer."

A bold claim, considering Rooney only has three novels to her name, all published in the last few years: *Conversations with Friends* (2017), *Normal People* (2018), and *Beautiful World, Where Are You* (2021). But to be fair, Flannery O'Connor wrote only two, *Wise Blood* and *The Violent Bear It Away*. Ditto for Powers, whose second novel, *Wheat That Springeth Green*, took him twenty-five years to write. So length of years or abundance of words aren't the only qualifiers to be a great Catholic writer.

Freeman noted that unlike the Irish literary giants of previous generations (Rooney's novels are all set in her native Ireland), "Rooney is writing within the context of a post-Catholic Ireland. She and her characters grew up in a world where the church's firm grasp on every aspect of life rapidly weakened after revelations of physical and sexual abuse." In a 2017 interview with the *Irish Times*, Rooney commented that "we got rid of the Catholic Church and replaced it with predatory capitalism. In some ways that was a good trade off, and in other ways, really bad."

After *Conversations with Friends* was published, the Irish public broadcasting network RTE called Rooney "Salinger for the Snapchat Generation." The *New York Times* noted in 2021 that Rooney's "popularity somehow eclipses the books themselves, her name an easy shorthand for a certain cultural sensibility, even to those who haven't read a word she's written."

Not everyone is a fan—Hillary Kelly savaged Rooney in the *Los Angeles Times* in 2021, describing her writing as "Hemingway simplicity cut with jabbering 'Gilmore Girls' erudition" and "bestselling fiction about bright young thinkers with their hands in each other's pants." Ouch.

But Rooney writes, Freeman noted, "for an audience that lacks faith in an institutional church, yet yearns for something to believe in. She writes for me and my friends." One of Rooney's characters in *Beautiful World, Where Are You*, Alice, says that "beauty, truth, and goodness are properties of being which are one with God." Catholic enough for you? It is a moment of straightforward catechism that might have come from the pen of St. Thomas Aquinas himself.

Rooney's second novel, *Normal People*, was made into a miniseries for Hulu in 2020. Freeman remembered that the literary buzz around Rooney's *Conversations with Friends* in 2017 made him worry about the quality of *Normal People*. "Rooney was marketed as Salinger for the Snapchat Generation, greeted as one of the first great millennial writers," he wrote, so he was nervous when her second novel was announced so soon after. "Sometimes a debut novelist will capitalize on her fame and rush to publish an inferior work, some old manuscript that had been shunted aside or buried deep on a hard drive."

Not so in this case. "It took me a while to realize that *Normal People* is not a watered down version of *Conversations with Friends*, but instead a smoothly refined sample of Rooney's writing."

One of the clearest examples of the sacramental sense that

infuses all of Rooney's writing comes from her presentation of our human corporeality in *Normal People*: "The Catholic imagination is latently present in the way that Rooney writes about the body," Freeman wrote, and her characters are no disembodied souls fleeing worldly experiences. "Their experience of God, of what is good, is rooted in each other and expressed through their bodies. Throughout the story they find mercy and grace and love through each other. Their bodies serve as extensions of their souls."

37

ANDRE DUBUS
Life's Terrors and Glories

We all probably have a favorite short story or novel about dads (no shade if it's *King Lear*, it happens), and my preparations for writing a column about Father's Day a few years back brought me back to a classic, one of the most haunting yet beautiful tales I have ever read about fatherhood (and Catholicism): Andre Dubus's "A Father's Story."

In the classroom, I would regularly use this story for one of the first class discussions with college students. A first-person account of a father who covers up a hit-and-run accident to protect his daughter, it takes the reader's certainties about morality and responsibility and sacrifice and turns them on their head. I once heard a spirituality professor tell students that Dubus's story was a "classic example of poor discernment," which, sure, whatever, but it's still a beautiful tale.

Fans of Dubus received a new chance to enjoy his work with a three-book re-release of his short stories in 2018; in his review of one volume, *The Winter Father*, Kevin Spinale, S.J., called Dubus a "writer of Old Testament clarity" and described "A Father's Story" as a tale "thick with insight into prayer and parental love." Spinale singled out the following passage from the story as some of Dubus's finest work:

When I received the Eucharist while Jennifer's car sat twice-damaged, so redeemed, in the rain, I felt neither loneliness nor shame, but as though He were watching me, even from my tongue, intestines, blood, as I have watched my sons at times in their young lives when I was able to judge but without anger, and so keep silent while they, in the agony of their youth, decided how they must act; or found reasons, after their actions, for what they had done. Their reasons were never as good or as bad as their actions, but they needed to find them, instead of the awful solitude of the heart.

In a review of all three volumes—*We Don't Live Here Anymore, The Winter Father,* and *The Cross Country Runner*—Franklin Freeman described Dubus as "an irascible, loyal, loving, smoking, hard-drinking, hard-punching, tender man, who demanded much of himself and others," and whose style was a cross between Chekhov and Hemingway.

Born in 1936 in Lake Charles, Louisiana, Dubus served in the Navy after college and then enrolled in the Iowa Writers Workshop, where he studied with Kurt Vonnegut and Richard Yates, among others. He taught for many years at Bradford College in Massachusetts, publishing novels, essays, and short stories all the while.

While trying to help a stranded motorist outside Boston in 1986, Dubus was hit by a car (a strange echo of the central action in "A Father's Story") and lost the use of both legs; with typical bluntness, he described himself for the rest of his life not as a paraplegic, but "a cripple." The accident also robbed him of a daily ritual—walking to morning Mass at the local parish.

His son Andre Dubus III is also a well-known author,

including the *New York Times* bestsellers *House of Sand and Fog*, *The Garden of Last Days*, and a memoir of his childhood, *Townie* (which makes it clear that his dad wasn't exactly father of the year for much of the son's life). "Because he wrote so well and deeply about the human condition, his editorial rejections were few and far between, as far as I know," Dubus's son told Freeman in a 2018 interview. "His biggest publishing challenge had more to do with his being a writer of short stories as opposed to the more commercial form, the novel." Father and son are not the only two writers in the extended family: Dubus's first cousin is the novelist James Lee Burke, himself the father of novelist Alafair Burke.

Patrick Samway, S.J., the author of *Walker Percy: A Life*, interviewed Dubus in 1986. The novelist had some harsh words for the American religious landscape. "I've seen the whole of my fictive world through the eyes of someone who believes the main problem in the United States is that we have lost all spiritual values and not replaced them with anything that is comparable. We just pretend all this. We never have been a Christian country," Dubus told Samway. He went on:

> As a matter of fact, there never has been a Christian country. Has there ever been a country that didn't kill its enemies, oppress the poor and bring the strong and the rich to power? Well, it saddens me and angers me. Maybe that's why I'm fascinated by the mystics, those who transcend all that drowns me. The mystics remain in harmony with the earth and their fellow human beings and, yet, are above it all as they enjoy union with God.

That desired union with God in a broken world lurks behind much of Dubus's fiction, with "A Father's Story" being a prime example. "The works of Andre Dubus are hard to read, even though they are beautifully written—combining the simplicity of Hemingway with the fullness and fluidity of Faulkner—because they face life and love so starkly," Franklin Freeman wrote in 2018. "Which is why, after almost every story and novella I read, I had to put the book down and wait before starting another. I had to let it settle into my soul before going on. And just that—the act of going on—is what Dubus encourages in us as we read him, to go on no matter how terrible and, in cyclical fashion, how glorious, life gets."

38

ANDRE DUBUS III
"Still, I Pray"

To be the writerly son of a writerly father is not always the easiest vocation. When that parent is as famous as Andre Dubus, it must be doubly difficult. Throw in the fact that Dubus *père* was by most accounts pretty bad at parenting, and you end up fishing in some dark waters indeed. But who knows: maybe it can make for great art?

One might ask Andre Dubus III. Dubus *fils* has managed to carve out an illustrious career as both a novelist and short story writer. Due to his father or in spite of him? Hard to say.

When Dubus III was ten years old and his other siblings still young, the elder Dubus left his wife and children for one of his writing students. As a result, the family of five "was forced to live in squalor on a diet of sodas and Frito casseroles in one cheap rented house after another in the failed mill town of Haverhill, Mass.," Ron Hansen wrote in his 2011 review of Dubus III's memoir, *Townie*. Meanwhile, the senior Dubus was "increasingly becoming an acclaimed writer of graceful, sensitive, acutely observed short stories during this period, but he was stunningly oblivious to what was happening to his abandoned children."

Though *Townie* can be a difficult read, Dubus III has said

157

in recent years that he does not necessarily hold too much ill will toward his father. "I'm no authority on forgiveness, but I do believe that my father, who was very young when he became a husband and a father, in his early twenties, did the best that he knew how to do at the time, which, of course, is not the same as doing the best he *could* do," he told Franklin Freeman in a 2018 interview. "This is true for all of us, though, isn't it? And that's where the potential for growth comes in. None of us are exempt from screwing up."

Dubus the younger simply believes his father, to paraphrase Yeats, chose the perfection of his work over the perfection of his life. "I believe strongly, and I have a hunch my father would agree with me on this, that in his 62 years on the planet, my father put the very best part of himself into his writing. Everything else, including his wife and children, came after that," Dubus III said. "A close second I would add. But after that." His father, who had been badly wounded in a car accident at fifty, died in 1999. He is profiled elsewhere in this book.

When he was just twenty-three, Dubus the younger published his first short story, "Forky" (no relation to the *Toy Story 4* character); it was followed seven years later by his short story collection, *The Cage Keeper and Other Stories*. He published his debut novel, *Bluesman*, in 1993.

Dubus III hit the big time with his 1999 novel, *House of Sand and Fog*, which was a finalist for the National Book Award, a *New York Times* bestseller, and an Oprah's Book Club selection to boot. Dubus also wrote the screenplay for the Academy Award–nominated film adaptation. It was followed by *The Garden of Last Days* in 2008, *Dirty Love* in 2013, *Gone So Long* in 2018, and now *Such Kindness*.

Dubus *fils* has also written his share of book reviews over the years. His 1989 review of Peter Matthiessen's sprawling short story collection, *On the River Styx,* is a writer's review in every sense of the word, focusing as much on Matthiessen's craft as on his characters or themes. Reading it, I felt like I was back in an M.F.A. workshop with a master teacher, one with an eye for a writer's gifts as well as follies. Dubus calls the title story "one of the most sophisticated in structure and scope, and purely focused on style." Another story is praised for "Matthiessen's stylistic strength: his descriptions of nature."

In a 1995 review of Alice Munro's *Open Secrets,* Dubus III quoted Nadine Gordimer on writing short stories: "Whether it sprawls or neatly bites its own tail . . . to write one is to express from a situation in the exterior or interior world the life-giving drop—sweat, tear, semen, saliva—that will spread with intensity on the page, burn a hole in it." He praised Munro for her "brilliant and unforgettable stories," ones that "manage not only to 'sprawl' but to also 'neatly bite their own tail.'" Among the elements for which his father's fiction was noted were its strongly Catholic themes. Did the father's faith affect his son? "While I personally do not believe in a God or some all-knowing, all-powerful entity who knows and cares about me, I do believe in the divine. I believe there is something invisible and maybe even benevolent in and around us at all times all our lives long," Dubus III told Freeman in 2018.

"Until my wife and I had our first child twenty-five years ago, I do not believe I had prayed even once. Though I have been doing it daily for years for our now three children. I am not an atheist, nor do I believe that anyone's listening either, but still, I pray."

39

JOAN DIDION
"In Sunlight or Loneliness"

"Joan Didion uses language and controls structure so artfully that from the welter of futile speech and action she dramatizes so vividly comes a clear statement on the human condition," wrote Elizabeth Woods Shaw in a 1977 review of Didion's novel *A Book of Common Prayer*. "The mirror she holds up to nature reflects crazily angled, grotesque images; but the reflections themselves are so sharp that watching them provides a rare aesthetic pleasure."

Didion, Shaw noted, was capable both of conjuring up the horrors of modern life and of offering solace that there was still a point to it all. "It is terrifying to be made to realize how high the flood of meaninglessness has risen beneath the familiar surface of life," she wrote of Didion's prose. "Yet, as long as an ordering intelligence can shape chaos into meaning in the very act of imitating it, we need not despair. The spirit is still moving over the waters."

When Joan Didion died on December 23, 2021, in New York City at the age of eighty-seven, the many obituaries and encomiums that followed noted her reliability as an observer—both in fiction and in reporting—but also her ability to bring her own idiosyncratic perspective to everything she wrote. It is perhaps no surprise, then, that such a representative of the "New Journalism," with its focus on unconventional literary technique and individual perspectives, grew up in California, the subject of much of her early writing and historically a place where, well, idiosyncrasy finds toleration—and more often than not, celebration.

I grew up in Southern California myself, and have always found the opening lines of Didion's 1964 essay "Los Angeles Notebook," later reprinted in her masterful *Slouching towards Bethlehem,* to be her finest writing—eerie and portentous but also rather matter-of-fact at the same time. She writes as a resident who is simultaneously an outsider. (Didion grew up in Sacramento, a quirky place too but an entirely different California from Los Angeles.) Here she is on the restless, hungry feeling caused by certain Southern California winds:

> There is something uneasy in the Los Angeles air this afternoon, some unnatural stillness, some tension. What it means is that tonight a Santa Ana will begin to blow, a hot wind from the northeast whining down through the Cajon and San Gorgonio Passes, blowing up sand storms out along Route 66, drying the hills and the nerves to flash point. For a few days now we will see smoke back in the canyons, and hear sirens in the night. I have neither heard nor read that a Santa Ana is due, but I know it, and almost everyone I have seen today knows it too. We know it because we feel it. The baby frets. The maid sulks. I rekindle a waning argument with the telephone company, then cut my losses and lie down, given over to whatever it is in the air. To

live with the Santa Ana is to accept, consciously or unconsciously, a deeply mechanistic view of human behavior.

A thing of beauty—and, in typical Didion fashion, it serves as an introduction to the story of a macabre and somewhat inexplicable Southern California murder. Did the supercharged ions in the wind bring felonious impulses with them? Or is our natural environment a convenient excuse for the disasters we all cause ourselves in life? That question can be found lurking underneath much of Didion's writing.

Her books—and those of her late husband, John Gregory Dunne, whose novel *True Confessions* is another masterpiece of writing about Los Angeles—were often reviewed in the pages of trade magazines as well as Catholic ones like *National Catholic Reporter, Commonweal,* and *America,* including her autobiographical accounts of dealing with the deaths of Dunne (*A Year of Magical Thinking*) and of their daughter, Quintana Roo (*Blue Nights*).

In his 2006 review of *A Year of Magical Thinking,* Bill Gunlocke notes Didion's courage and fortitude in making her own grief the object of her investigation; she was a new widow but nevertheless still the inquisitive reporter. "As she has always done, she burrows into the piles of details to learn about what happened. She works to learn the language of emergency rooms and autopsies. She asks the apartment building's elevator operator what he remembers. She retraces that night and the death that occurred. She talks to herself and puts quotation marks around her words," he writes. "She lets the readers in, so that they grasp her solitude and loss in ways they had never thought about such solitude and loss before, and in ways Didion hadn't either."

Didion's recollections of the life she and Dunne shared—"the California homes, the meals with literary friends and movie people, the dinners with just the two of them together, the swimming pools, the travels, the clothes"—are all "recollections that evoke a mood, an atmosphere," Gunlocke wrote. "She gives the reader what the reader appreciates most. That is what makes even Joan Didion's sad tale somehow stimulating to read. Wherever she finds herself, be it in sunlight or loneliness, her experience is palpable to the reader, who is transported to where she is—and wants to be there with her."

In a 2012 review of *Blue Nights*, Bill Williams notes that Didion's constant rumination on what it means to age (and to die) gave her prose a heavy weight in her autobiographical works, including her reflections on the life and death of her adopted daughter, Quintana Roo. (In case you're wondering, her name comes from the Mexican state.) Roo had a difficult adult life, as she was diagnosed variously with manic depression, obsessive-compulsive disorder, and borderline personality disorder. She died of pancreatitis at thirty-nine after what Didion called a "cascade of medical crises."

"Didion ponders Quintana's life and death in spare prose that is at once insightful, depressing, and random. The book is as much a meditation on the author's own fear of aging and illness as it is a lament about the loss of an only child," Williams wrote.

In *Blue Nights*, Didion herself concedes she has spent much of her life in denial of aging. "Only yesterday," she writes, "I could still do arithmetic, remember telephone numbers, rent a car at the airport and drive it out of the lot without freezing, stopping at the key moment, feet already on the pedals but immobilized by the question of which is the accelerator and which the brake." But at seventy-seven, having lost her husband and daughter, she finds herself losing even the creative powers that made her so successful as a writer. And yet she chronicles this loss, too, confessing that her "cognitive confidence seems to have vanished altogether."

Perhaps most remarkable about Didion is that these autobiographical works were hardly what she was known for best; rather it was her essay collections, her reporting on places like El Salvador and Miami, her screenplays and her many forays into fiction that earned her fame. She could make anything intriguing, including herself.

40

C. S. Lewis
Savvy Apologetics

The 2023 Christmas release *Freud's Last Session* is an imagined meeting between Sigmund Freud and C. S. Lewis at the outbreak of World War II. Adapted from a 2009 play by Mark St. Germain, the dialogue-heavy movie didn't do well with critics, even though Anthony Hopkins won plaudits for his depiction of Freud (weird coincidence, as Hopkins depicted Lewis in the biopic *Shadowlands* in 1993). On the other hand, noted a friend, "Freud got all the best lines."

Then again, so did Screwtape. The clever title character of Lewis's fiction classic *The Screwtape Letters* was also an expert in psychology, as well as one of Satan's most promising demons. Screwtape isn't Freud, of course, and Freud isn't Screwtape, but one can see that even Lewis knew that talking about life's temptations is a little sexier for most readers than portraying the paths to holiness.

Indeed, Lewis is an acquired taste—sometimes a reacquired taste. I fell in love with his *Narnia* and *Space Trilogy* novels as a kid, but didn't much enjoy his apologetic works like *Mere Christianity* or *God in the Dock* that I read as an adult. Lewis can feel like an Anglican G. K. Chesterton in those books, and like most people of goodwill, I can't stand G. K. Chesterton.

In later years, however, encounters with Lewis's more autobiographical works like *A Grief Observed* and *Surprised by Joy* brought me back into the fold and reminded me why Lewis is such a beloved spiritual writer. In the historian Mark Noll's book *C. S. Lewis in America*, he suggests that Lewis became so popular on this side of the pond for particular reasons: "Americans saw Lewis as *deeply learned, theologically focused*, and *unusually creative*. Implicitly, they also recognized that his articulation of the faith was savvy and courageous." Those qualities are worth a thousand smug Chestertonianisms.

Born in Belfast in 1898, Clive Staples Lewis ("Jack" to family and friends, as viewers of *Freud's Last Session* will be reminded) was primarily a scholar of English literature by trade. Wounded in the trenches of France during World War I, he studied at Oxford after the war and became a professor there in 1925, teaching at Oxford for almost thirty years and at Cambridge for nine more before he died in 1963. (As an Irishman, he had many clever and acid observations of his British academic peers over the years.)

Though raised in the Church of Ireland, Lewis became an atheist as a young man, returning to Christianity only in his thirties. Lewis was influenced in his return to the faith by his new friend J. R. R. Tolkien, a fellow Inkling in that distinguished group of Oxford storytellers and scholars and professors at Oxford; another influence, it seems, was the aforementioned G. K. Chesterton. In 1956, Lewis married the American Joy Davidman. Her death in 1960 spurred Lewis to write *A Grief Observed* about his experience of loss and mourning. Lewis had published the book under a pseud-onym and soon found friends unknowingly gifting him his own book as valuable spiritual reading to deal with his loss.

Though his *Narnia* books are his bestsellers by far (and have been adapted for radio, stage, and screen), Lewis also wrote scholarly tomes, other novels like *The Great Divorce*, and numerous books of nonfiction, such as popular collections of essays and talks, including *The Abolition of Man* and *Mere Christianity*, as well as other apologetic works like *Miracles* and *The Problem of Pain*. *The Screwtape Letters* remains perhaps his funniest, most light-hearted, and most clever work and has been imitated by more than a few writers, believers or not.

From the start Lewis had many fans on this side of the pond, even for his early (and widely panned) 1936 novel, *Pilgrim's Regress*. One reviewer that year praised it for its "correctness of fact that is not lessened by fancy, epigrammatic bits of wisdom, an argument spicy and not insipid, subtle yet easily caught." In 1944, Charles Brady praised *The Screwtape Letters* as not just a work of theological brilliance but as an imaginative twin of Lewis Carroll's finest work. "Not since another Oxford don chose to divest himself of his academic robes and slip down a rabbit-hole with Alice and the White Rabbit has the reading world been given such a divertissement by a race of spectacled savants," Brady wrote.

Though his primary American audience has always been evangelical Protestants, the turmoil following the Second Vatican Council also seemed to give Lewis a newfound popularity among Catholic writers, perhaps for his seeming implacability in the face of rapidly changing mores and practices. "C. S. Lewis is as refreshing as a sea breeze. In a time when men are not always what their images project, to meet the blatantly honest and open C. S. Lewis is a delight," wrote Thomas M. Sheehan in 1970 in a review of a collection of Lewis's works. "Lewis is a man willing to declare himself a believer in God; willing to state that any unanswerable questions about God will be resolved in heaven," he wrote. "For Lewis, God is real, and so, for that matter, is Satan; there is a heaven, and there is a hell."

In 2019, the spiritual writer Jessica Mesman wrote of the profound ways in which Lewis's *A Grief Observed* not only helped her through a time of prolonged suffering but also reminded her of why she became a writer in the first place. In that book, she wrote, a newly widowed Lewis is "disgusted by the platitudes of well-meaning religious friends and the sympathy cards—he calls them 'pitiable cant.'" Lewis will have none of it—if the joys of life are worth being cherished and celebrated, so too must the sufferings of life be reckoned with honestly:

> *A Grief Observed* remains powerful precisely because Lewis does not come to lovely conclusions about his God or his religion or his suffering. He asks many more questions than he answers. He rants, questions, weeps and feels terrible, deservedly sorry for himself and for the woman he loved so much and has now lost. And in doing so, he renders in prose what it really feels like to grieve.

Fifty years after his death, C. S. Lewis was recognized at "Poet's Corner" in Westminster Abbey, where many famous English-language writers are buried or honored. His stepson Douglas Gresham read a passage from *The Last Battle* from Lewis's *Narnia* series at the service. The inscription on the

stone floor of the church honoring Lewis is a quote from one
of his talks:

> I believe in Christianity as I believe that the Sun has
> risen, not only because I see it but because by it I see
> everything else.

41

WALTER CISZEK
Tougher Than You

On a trip to rural Pennsylvania in May 2022, I had the chance to stop by the Jesuit Center in Wernersville, a few miles outside of Reading. Built in 1930 to serve as a novitiate for the Maryland Province of the Society of Jesus, the 250-acre property features a huge (eighty-five bedrooms!) central building as well as lawns, grottoes, terraces, and more—including a cemetery for Maryland Province Jesuits. It was there that I finally got to visit the grave of Walter Ciszek, S.J.

It is impossible to read Walter Ciszek's life story and not want to have met him. He will likely one day be canonized a saint (at the moment he is a "Servant of God," an important first step in a long process, and his cause for canonization is now under the auspices of the Diocese of Allentown) for his heroic life of service, including twenty-four years in the Soviet Union, most of which were spent in prison or in the infamous gulag system of labor camps.

A tough kid from Shenandoah, Pennsylvania, he surprised his family and friends when he entered a local seminary after high school (apparently he had been in a local gang as a teen). At the age of twenty-four, he entered the Jesuits. Ordained in 1937 after time in Rome to study theology and learn Russian, he was sent to Poland in 1938. When the Soviet Union occupied Eastern Poland in the early stages of the Second World War, Ciszek snuck into Russia under an assumed name and ministered to Catholics in the Ural Mountains (he had been ordained for both the Roman Catholic and the Byzantine rite) while working as a logger.

In 1941, Ciszek was arrested and accused of spying for the Vatican. He spent five years in Moscow's notorious Lubyanka prison, much of it in solitary confinement, and he then was sent to Siberia to work in forced labor camps throughout the region. As Ciszek related in his two memoirs, *With God in Russia* and *He Leadeth Me*, he also clandestinely ministered as a priest during years working in coal mines and factories. His family and religious community in the United States presumed he was dead, with the Jesuits including his name among deceased Jesuits for whom they prayed in 1947.

In 1955, Ciszek was released from the gulag (and succeeded in contacting his sisters back home) even as he was still closely monitored by the KGB and was forced to remain in the Soviet Union, where he worked for years as an auto mechanic while also continuing to minister as a priest. Finally, in 1963, the Soviet Union agreed to release Ciszek and another American who had been convicted of spying in exchange for the release of Ivan and Aleksandra Egorov, two Soviet nationals accused of the same in the United States. His arrival in New York City drew national attention. Five months later, he related the moment:

> My plane landed at Idlewild International Airport, at 6:55 A.M., in the gray dawn of October 12, 1963. All during the long flight from Moscow, I had wondered what it would be like to see the United States again

after 24 years in the Soviet Union, mostly in Siberia. Yet, as we taxied to the terminal, I forgot all about that; I could think only of my sisters and of the fellow Jesuits I saw waiting to meet me. My throat seemed somehow to grow suddenly tighter; I felt a nervous happiness in the expectancy of that first meeting. I hardly remember much about Idlewild, therefore, except flashing lights in the early dawn, the crowd of reporters and that feeling of joy at being home. It was a long while before I could even begin to sift out my impressions of things here.

Among those there to meet Ciszek were his sisters and three Jesuits, including Thurston N. Davis, S.J., the editor in chief of *America*. Davis remembered the moment later, joking that "in his green raincoat, grey suit, and big-brimmed Russian felt hat, Fr. Ciszek looked like the movie version of a stocky little Soviet member of an agricultural mission." Davis drove him home from the airport. "We tried to shake an unknown man in a cab who tailed us," Davis remembered, "but he followed us to our door and then drove away."

Later that day, Ciszek was driven out to Wernersville to escape the droves of reporters and to be near his family home. One tale—perhaps apocryphal—is that the Jesuits had a secondary motive for the trip. They couldn't be entirely sure the man in the green raincoat was actually Walter Ciszek; no one had seen him in twenty-four years, and he had been at hard labor for most of that time. Was the man before them actually a Soviet sleeper agent? As the story goes, he was driven around the Wernersville property with a former classmate who periodically asked him questions: What's over this next hill? What will we see when we pass this grotto? Where is the well located? No Soviet spy could possibly know the lay of that land. He passed the test.

Daniel Flaherty, S.J., worked with Ciszek on writing his memoirs. For six months after Ciszek's return, they worked together to get his story onto paper. "It was not a hard story to write," Flaherty remembered. "Walter had a fantastic memory, and my only job was to get it down on paper." Unfortunately, they were a bit too prolific: When they finally finished the manuscript in March 1964, it was 1,500 pages long. They went back to work, and by that summer had it down to 500.

With God in Russia almost instantly gained recognition as a spiritual classic and remains in print today. It was followed in 1973 by *He Leadeth Me*, also co-written with Flaherty. After the books were written, Ciszek worked for many years in ecumenical relations and exchanges with Eastern churches. He died in 1984.

His writings in both memoirs and elsewhere can be challenging: He was not overjoyed by everything he saw of the United States upon his return. He found American society shockingly wasteful, noting that "I've watched mothers in the kitchen after a meal throw away more food, and better food, than I might eat in Russia in half a week." He was also dismayed to see how cavalier many Americans were about faith: "At first glance religion here seems almost a formality, an obligation that can be dispensed with if you have been out late the night before," he said. "I could not help being struck, thunderstruck, at this initial impression of indifference to religion in a country where there was nothing to restrain its open practice."

Perhaps after twenty-four years, he felt he had a right to speak his mind.

42

Brian Moore
The Precarity of Faith

October 19 is the "Memorial of Saints John de Brébeuf and Isaac Jogues, Priests, and Companions, Martyrs" in the Catholic lectionary for Mass used in the United States. Those of us south of the Canadian border might know them better as the "American Martyrs," while those on the other side prefer the "Canadian Martyrs" and celebrate their feast day on September 26. If you're in a Jesuit parish or ministry, you'll probably hear "North American Martyrs," a clever way to sidestep the problem of the overweening jingoism of our neighbors to the north.

In mainstream U.S. culture, those martyrs are perhaps best remembered because of *Black Robe*, a 1985 novel by Brian Moore that was later turned into a 1991 film by the same name, directed by Bruce Beresford (Moore wrote the screenplay). Both the book and movie relate the fictionalized experiences of a group of French Jesuit missionaries sent to "New France" to work primarily with the Huron Nation in the interior of Canada in the seventeenth century.

Those missionaries were based on six Jesuit priests from France (Isaac Jogues, Antoine Daniel, Jean de Brébeuf, Gabriel Lalemant, Charles Garnier, and Noël Chabanel) and two *donnés,* lay assistants (René Goupil and Jean de la Lande), who were all martyred between 1642 and 1649. The tales of their exploits (and martyrdom) were published at home in France in *The Relations of the Jesuits of New France.* Isaac Jogues in particular became famous for coming home after having been tortured and mutilated—then returning to New France to try again and ultimately meet his fate. Canonized in 1930, the North American Martyrs are honored today at a number of shrines in the United States and Canada and in numerous hagiographies.

But why would their stories inspire a Belfast-born Irishman with no great love for the Catholic Church? Brian Moore seems an unlikely candidate to write hagiography at first glance. Born in 1921 into a Catholic family of nine children in Belfast, Northern Ireland, Moore spent most of his career in exile from both his homeland and his childhood faith, living in Canada and California and writing (in over two dozen novels, as well as short stories and screenplays) often of the Catholic Church's negative impact on Irish life, the pernicious influence of the priesthood on religion, and the general precarity of faith entirely. He described himself over the years as "agnostic" or "not religious."

At the same time, a number of Moore's novels dealt subtly and deftly with the profound emotional impact of struggles with faith, including *Catholics,* a 1972 novel called a "near masterpiece" by the *New York Times.* That short book might be perhaps the greatest poke in the eye of the post–Second Vatican Council church ever written—the tale of an Irish monastery that clings to a pre-Vatican II liturgy and spirituality in a Catholic Church lost in the throes of a syncretist "Vatican IV." (There was a 1973 made-for-TV movie adaptation, starring Martin Sheen, in his *Apocalypse Now* days.) A reviewer of the book in 1973 wrote that "if reading it upsets you, do not be surprised. With one stroke Moore has eliminated our standard escape from God—a secularized Kingdom or a romanticized past."

Seventeen years before, Moore's breakthrough novel, *The Lonely Passion of Judith Hearne,* had presented "the portrait of a soul seeking to expand, seeking to find faith, mercy, and companionship," in the words of Kevin Spinale, S.J., in a 2017 reflection on "Three Little-Known Catholic Novels That Can Enrich Your Faith." Thirteen years later, *Black Robe,* with its tormented priests trying to find both meaning and comfort in a harsh and foreign land, marked a return to what John Breslin, S.J., called "these troubling questions of faith and the transcendent" with which Moore's fiction dealt for much of the rest of his career.

"For all his suspicions about faiths and allegiances, he could never stop worrying them, especially in their religious, and usually Catholic, forms," wrote Breslin. "From his earliest and best known novel, *The Lonely Passion of Judith Hearne,* to his last, *The Magician's Wife,* the mystery of belief has haunted his best fiction."

In a 2006 essay, James Martin, S.J., included the film adaptation of *Black Robe* among his "10 best films and documentaries about the saints." Martin found Moore's story inspiring even if strikingly unsentimental. "Some Catholics find this movie, based on the stark novel by Brian Moore (who also wrote the screenplay), unpleasant for its bleak portrayal of the life of the priest as well as for its implicit critique that the missionaries brought only misfortune to the Indians," Martin wrote. "But, in the end, the movie offers a man who strives to bring God to the people that he ends up loving deeply. The final depiction of the answer to the question,

'Blackrobe, do you love us?' attempts to sum up an entire Catholic tradition of missionary work."

Breslin also regarded *Black Robe* as Moore's masterpiece, noting that the efforts of the main character, Father Laforgue, "to cling to an absolute of conscience in the face of intolerable physical pain, spiritual despair, and failure triggers the literary adrenalin." At the same time, Moore escaped the pitfalls of hagiography in his rather bleak tale, giving Father Laforgue a vitality that places him among the most compelling priests of twentieth-century Catholic fiction.

"Moore's conviction . . . that love trumps all other spiritual values, is consonant, ironically, with the deepest truth of the Gospel and with a soupy humanistic sentimentalism," Breslin wrote. "What saves it here and elsewhere is the crucible of passionate commitment and intense suffering from which it emerges. Thus Laforgue joins the other renegade clerics of twentieth-century Catholic fiction: Greene's whiskey priest, Bernanos's curé, Endo's Jesuit missionary. Not bad company for character or novelist."

43

L. C. McHugh
Aquinas and the Fallout Shelter

Every now and then, usually in the basement of a public building or school, one can still stumble across a relic of another era: three yellow triangles within a black circle. It signifies a fallout shelter.

What is a fallout shelter, you might wonder? If you need to ask, it means you're younger than a certain age, as fallout shelters were once a national craze in the United States. But it is true that they have all but disappeared from our consciousness. Why? It's a long story, and a wonky priest is a big part of it.

As the Cold War seemed close to going hot in the early 1960s, the question of how to protect the civilian population from a Soviet nuclear attack was a commonly debated one. (And no, getting under your desk at school wasn't going to work.) While politicians debated the cost and effectiveness of public fallout shelters, a huge industry emerged providing private shelters to American homeowners.

In August 1961, *Time* magazine ran a story on the phenomenon of Americans stockpiling weapons in such shelters to protect themselves against less-well-prepared neighbors who might seek entrance when the bombs began to fall:

"Gun Thy Neighbor?" The article concluded with reactions from clergy of different Christian denominations, almost all of whom expressed an uneasiness with the idea of barring others from one's own family shelter, with one minister declaring that "if someone wanted to use the shelter, then you yourself should get out and let him use it. That's not what would happen, but that's the strict Christian application."

Enter L. C. McHugh, S.J., a Jesuit priest and a former ethics professor from Georgetown University. McHugh took objection to the quote above in an essay for *America* on September 31, 1961, titled "Ethics at the Shelter Doorway."

"I cannot accept that statement as it stands," he wrote. "It argues that we must love our neighbor, not as ourselves, but more than ourselves." It was important, McHugh noted, to remember and apply traditional Christian principles of self-defense to the question of "gunning one's neighbor at the shelter door." Those principles, he argued, made it clear that every shelter owner had a right to defend his or her shelter for the use of family and friends—and that there was no moral prohibition against using deadly force to do so.

McHugh continued in blunt terms. "If a man builds a shelter for his family, then it is the family that has the first right to use it. The right becomes empty if a misguided charity prompts a pitying householder to crowd his haven to the hatch in the hour of peril; for this conduct makes sure that no one will survive," he wrote. "And I consider it the height of nonsense to say that the Christian ethic demands or even permits a man to thrust his family into the rain of fallout when unsheltered neighbors plead for entrance."

Further, he wrote, "If you are already secured in your shelter and others try to break in, they may be treated as unjust aggressors and repelled with whatever means will effectively deter their assault. If others steal your family shelter space before you get there, you may also use whatever means will recover your sanctuary intact."

Was McHugh being entirely serious, or was the whole thing a kind of Swiftian modest proposal, a satire designed to horrify those who were up until then supporting fallout shelters? In truth, his author biography for the article stated that "Our guess is that Fr. McHugh would be the first to step aside from his own shelter door, yielding space to his neighbor."

And indeed, the article did not bolster the fallout shelter industry, but tolled its death knell: a bit of a media frenzy followed its publication, with everyone from the *New York Times* to the national wire services reporting on it and reactions coming from all quarters, most of them condemnatory. The repugnance many readers felt toward McHugh's argument seemed to trigger a national reckoning with the unspoken assumptions of fallout shelters and their moral significance.

McHugh doubled down two months after his initial article, writing "More on the Shelter Question" for the November 25, 1961, issue of *America* and asking "a series of rather excruciating questions" about the morality of fallout shelters. While admitting his analyses "took a somewhat technical approach to a crisis of conscience," he nevertheless laid out some of the moral dilemmas both citizens and governments could face in the event of a nuclear war.

Many public Christian figures were aghast, suggesting McHugh had lost his moral compass. The preeminent Protestant theologian Reinhold Niebuhr accused him of "justifying murder." Writing in *Time*, the Episcopal bishop of Washington, Bishop Angus Dun, called McHugh's position "utterly immoral." Eventually even Billy Graham weighed in, saying he was against the construction of private fallout shelters.

The private shelter–building craze died out over the next few years, with many Americans seeming to punt the project to the federal government or to prefer not thinking about the aftermath of the unthinkable. Well, until recently.

McHugh's article even reached the desks of those at the highest levels of government. In Arthur Schlesinger Jr.'s *A Thousand Days*, he recounts a discussion of public fallout shelters among Kennedy administration officials at Hyannis Port in 1961 that included a sour comment from Attorney General Robert F. Kennedy: "There's no problem here—we can just station Father McHugh with a machine gun at every shelter."

44

Colm Tóibín
Exile

When *A Guest at the Feast* by Colm Tóibín was released in early 2024, fans were no doubt pleased that Tóibín had brought together many of his essays in a single book, reflecting on themes and topics that have made the Irish wordsmith one of the preeminent authors in the English-speaking world. Americans might best know him from his novel *Brooklyn*, but for thirty-two years he has been steadily publishing fiction, nonfiction, poetry, and plays.

Born in Enniscorthy, County Wexford, in Ireland (from which several of his fictional protagonists hail) in 1955, Tóibín moved to Barcelona in 1975 after graduating from University College Dublin. He lived in Spain until 1978, returning to Dublin and working as a writer and editor. His first novel, *The South*, was published in 1990.

To this point he has published eleven novels and two short story collections and has authored or edited more than twenty nonfiction volumes. A number of his novels have won or been finalists for prominent literary awards, particularly 1999's *The Blackwater Lightship*, 2004's *The Master*, 2009's *Brooklyn*, and his controversial 2012 *The Testament of Mary*. His 2021 novel *The Magician* was a portrait of the writer

Thomas Mann and his family, followed by 2024's *Long Island*, awaited by fans of his earlier *Brooklyn*.

A Guest at the Feast—a collection of previously published essays—gives us Tóibín's sharp takes on a number of topics and themes he has embraced before in both fiction and non, including the relationship between parents and children, how writers develop their themes in early life, the experience of growing up and living as a gay man in Ireland, his own 2018 bout with cancer (with a memorable first line: "It all started with my balls."), the love/hate relationship the Irish have with the Catholic Church, what it is like to be an exile, and more.

Tóibín's fictional characters can be dark—in his 2006 short story collection, *Mothers and Sons*, the protagonist believes "that behind everything lay something else, a hidden motive perhaps, or something unimaginable and dark, that a person was merely a disguise for another person, that something said was merely a code for something else," but they are always carefully detailed and multifaceted. The protagonist of *Brooklyn*, Eilis Lacy, is a simple woman from Enniscorthy when we first meet her; by the end of the novel she is one of the most psychologically complex and nuanced characters in recent literature, and her story continues with *Long Island*.

"As an artist, Tóibín is a traditional storyteller, so sure a stylist that he pares his words to the minimum, so confident a plot-master that he can end a story without resolving the plot yet leave a reader fully satisfied," wrote Joseph J. Feeney, S.J., in a 2012 review of *Mothers and Sons*.

Tóibín's 2012 novella *The Testament of Mary* compelled a number of commentaries in the Catholic press, some more nervous than others. The narrator of the book is Mary the mother of Jesus, speaking long after Good Friday, and she guides the reader through her life with Jesus as well as her own existence as an aging woman in Ephesus surrounded by disciples of Jesus, whom she describes as "my protectors, or my guards, or whatever it is they are," as Michael O'Loughlin noted in a 2012 essay.

This is no silent and passive Mary, but a mother with complex feelings toward her son and his followers. She is by turns angry, bitter, resigned, or unsure of her own recollections and convictions. Jesus's friends, wrote Diane Scharper in a 2012 review of the book, "want to invent a new religion that would establish her son as divine. But Mary won't accept that."

Instead, "Mary spends most of her time wondering whether she ever knew her son. When he was little, they were close, but then he fell in with a crowd of misfits. He became emotionally distant. She heard rumors that he healed a cripple and walked on water, but she can't believe that such actions could be performed by the boy she raised," Scharper wrote.

In a 2013 review of a play based on Tóibín's novella, Angela Alaimo O'Donnell praised Tóibín for "trying to deconstruct the images of the passive, bloodless Mary that dominated pietistic art of the 19th and 20th centuries," but also confessed that "much as I admire his writing, I could not countenance his Mary." What troubled O'Donnell? "After her son is nailed to the cross—a scene described in agonizing detail—Mary runs away. She runs away because she cannot help him, because she is afraid and (here is the hardest part to swallow) because she wants to save her own skin," she wrote.

No mother would run away while her son was being tortured and murdered, she argued—making Tóibín's depiction of Mary as difficult to believe as any pious rendering in art: "The inventions of tradition and bad art have provided us with too many impossible Marys who bear no relation to us," she continued. "Do we need another? Tóibín denies Mary what makes her most human, sinning at last against the law of verisimilitude, and giving us one more Mary we cannot believe in."

Also in 2013, Francis X. Clooney, S.J., proposed Tóibín's Mary as a good example of how the early Christians developed and defined their faith in an interreligious world. After all, Tóibín depicts Mary as visiting the temple of Artemis in Ephesus and talking with the Greek goddess. "Tóibín is unlikely to win any awards from the Church, or find his book for sale in the Vatican bookshop. He is, to be sure, not a Catholic theologian," Clooney wrote. "But in the whole of the book, and in these brief moments where Artemis is mentioned, he perhaps catches something of an experience we need not entirely rule out in our own meditations on Mary."

Why? Because even if "we for the most part accept the slow growth of Christian consciousness in the earliest Church, and even if we recognize, in theory at least, how it took a long time for the Gospels to be composed and finalized, perhaps we still are too confident about what this early period must have been like for those closest to Jesus, those who loved him most," Clooney continued.

"So Mary is now the patron of interreligious humility and learning? Perhaps too much of a claim to make," Clooney wrote. "But read *The Testament* and see what you think about Mary there, in the beginning, and Cana, and Artemis, when the mystery of Jesus was still stark and raw, and the Church had not yet found its language about its boundaries. At least imagine the possibilities before saying no."

45

MARY McGRORY
Washington's Best Writer

She won the Pulitzer Prize. She dated JFK. She was on Richard Nixon's enemies list. She wrote more than eight thousand columns on politics between 1954 and 2003. And she was a regular contributor to Catholic journals in the 1950s and 1960s: Mary McGrory.

"Washington Front" was a recurring column in *America* from the 1950s onward, usually offering Catholic takes on public policy but also sometimes just reporting on the nitty-gritty of the political game. Of the various authors who penned the column, none was better suited for the role than McGrory. She lived among Washington's power brokers and knew them all, which made for a life full of intriguing anecdotes and surprising historical moments—and a literary style all her own.

The first in her family to graduate college, McGrory eventually became one of the most popular syndicated columnists in the country, with over 150 newspapers running her musings on politics at the peak of her fame. She was widely admired for her willingness to wear out her shoe leather in her reporting and for her vast range of sources, and universally feared for her merciless pen.

Lyndon Johnson once complained that "Mary McGrory is the best writer in Washington, and she keeps getting better and better at my expense." Truth be told, Johnson got off easy. When Richard Nixon lost the California gubernatorial race in 1962, McGrory described his departure as "exit snarling." She once described Bill Clinton as a "lusty, scrape-prone lad." Of Ronald Reagan, she said he was a resolute believer in "making life more comfortable for the comfortable." The 2000 presidential race between Al Gore and George W. Bush? "A battle between the unlikable and the unprepared."

Like all journalists of proper upbringing, McGrory started out writing book reviews, first for the *Boston Herald* and then for the *Washington Star*, where she was hired as a literary editor in 1947. Her big break came in 1954, when her daily reports on the McCarthy hearings in Washington made her the talk of the town. McGrory, who never married or had children, reported later that her editors gave her that and other assignments on the condition she not get married.

"She was solidly progressive, quick to take up lost causes and not afraid to tackle abusive authority," wrote Tom Fox in a review of John Norris's 2016 biography, *Mary McGrory: The First Queen of Journalism.* "There was also both a predictability and unpredictability to her columns; you knew from where she was coming but not always where she was going."

McGrory stayed at the *Washington Star* until it folded in 1981, after which she moved to the *Washington Post.* In 1975, her coverage of Watergate earned her the Pulitzer Prize for commentary. She continued writing until she suffered a stroke in 2003. She died in 2004 at the age of eighty-five.

A Boston-born Catholic and a political liberal, McGrory was a great admirer of President John F. Kennedy and devoted many of her "Washington Front" columns to his political campaigns and his short presidency. Her 1961 column after Kennedy's inauguration (after an eight-inch snowfall) gave a sense of her admiration for him, whom she had first met in 1946 and dated briefly when he was a junior congressman.

"For those who struggled through the storm and braved the cold, there were rewards, chief among them which was the sight of the new young Chief Executive relishing every minute of the rites and the revels," she wrote, adding that "Mr. Kennedy was equal to it all. He stayed at the long and rather pretentious Inaugural Gala arranged by his friend Frank Sinatra until 1:30 in the morning, and made a speech of thanks at that hour. The next day in the bitter cold he stood at the top of the Capitol steps and delivered an Inaugural address that struck sparks with his frozen listeners."

A year earlier, she offered prescient reporting on Kennedy's attempt to woo voters in West Virginia, where anti-Catholic prejudice ran high. "The expressions on the faces of the Kennedy staff during the last week here were a measure of their dismay in being confronted by such a seemingly unscalable wall," she wrote in May 1960. However, Kennedy's appearance on television on the Sunday night before the primary— where he said he would not take instructions from the pope—turned the tide, McGrory wrote.

> The conquest of prejudice, however, means that Senator Kennedy need no longer name his religion as an obstacle to nomination. More than that, as he said at an early morning press conference at his jubilant headquarters in Charleston: "I think that, after the campaign in this State, it will not be necessary to mention it again." All present would certainly say a fervent "amen" to that.

Six months later, the United States elected its first Catholic president.

McGrory was deeply affected by Kennedy's assassination in 1963. Her reaction to the news—and Daniel Patrick Moynihan's response—have become the stuff of legend. "We'll never laugh again," McGrory is reported to have said in the aftermath. "Heavens, Mary," Moynihan replied. "We'll laugh again. It's just that we will never be young again."

John Norris, the author of the aforementioned biography of McGrory, wrote in 2015 that though "Ms. McGrory's faith was largely absent from her columns (she objected to proselytizing), it shaped her far more than most of her readers, and even many of her friends, appreciated. Her faith was her moral center."

Though McGrory lamented Pope Paul VI's promulgation of *Humanae Vitae*, prohibiting the use of artificial birth control ("to be a Catholic doesn't mean to be an imbecile"), she was strongly pro-life, and she objected to what she saw as a view among Democrats "that every single intelligent person is pro-abortion."

McGrory was also famous for her philanthropic ventures, especially her work at St. Ann's, a Washington orphanage—and for her strong-arm tactics to get Washington elites to volunteer or donate to her favorite charities. (Maureen Dowd once described her as "she who must be obeyed.") Tom Fox thought some of her work on behalf of the marginalized was inspired by the blatant sexism and discrimination she herself had faced in her career: "I think McGrory, who had to fight a woman's way to the table, overturning old habits, ended up also more sympathetic to others who remained excluded."

46

WILLIAM LYNCH
Isn't It Ironic?

Any study of Catholic intellectuals of the twentieth century will inevitably include names like John Courtney Murray, Elizabeth Johnson, Walter Ong, Avery Dulles, Margaret Farley, and more (sorry, no Bernard Lonergan, he was Canadian). But what if I told you that there was another scholar, a friend of Murray, whose writings on everything from theater to fiction to politics to civil society to mental health were equally as important at the time? A man of great intellect and insight, he still today lacks the reputation he deserves: William F. Lynch, S.J.

I will admit I am biased; in the summer of 2011, I had the opportunity to do a directed study of Lynch under John F. Kane, a Regis University professor and an expert on Lynch, who published a hefty intellectual biography of him, *Building the Human City*, in 2016. I got to read much of Lynch's work and discuss it with Kane, including Lynch's classic books *The Image Industries, Christ and Apollo, Images of Hope*, and *Images of Faith*.

I suspect the biggest obstacle to Lynch's rising to the prominence that his work deserved is that he had *too many* interests, all of which he approached with somewhat digres-

190

sive movements that avoided the declarative in favor of the descriptive.

Though trained as a philosopher, Lynch emphasized concrete and contextualized experiences throughout his writings. The attempt to escape from time, from embodied realities, from personal and societal movement and development, Lynch wrote, was an aesthetic and spiritual disaster, both for Western culture and for individuals. Think of the incarnation of Christ, Lynch writes in *Images of Faith*; what the Christian believes to be the most important moment in all creation occupies one tiny moment in fourteen billion years of space-time. If Christ can be born in a situation of such sheer irony (an important concept for Lynch), should that not be a reminder that we cannot and should not try to escape our historical milieus or the context in which we exist?

Lynch also advanced the notion of the analogical imagination—a way of looking at the world as being suffused with and analogous to an infinite divine reality—years before similar concepts were championed by David Tracy and Andrew Greeley. One of his biggest fans was Flannery O'Connor for almost precisely this reason: every human beauty, for Lynch as well as for O'Connor, points toward and is referent to a divine, transcendental beauty. In 2015, the O'Connor scholar Mark Bosco, S.J., noted that "Father Lynch's work validated O'Connor's particular modernist, even postmodernist proclivities and her own artistic claim to a Christic imagination." For both, "finite and infinite realities coalesce; so for Father Lynch, as for O'Connor, there is no need to pull together what has never been separated."

Kane's book, the first comprehensive biography of Lynch, also addresses Lynch's lifelong examination of contemporary society through the use of various images in his writings and talks. In a 2016 review of *Building the Human City*, Brett McLaughlin, S.J., quoted Kane's recognition that instead of seeking "a systematic or fundamental perspective on Catholic life in the United States," Lynch instead was "in all he wrote concerned to understand, and to help us understand, a number of basic ideas which he saw as crucial or foundational for ability to respond to the challenges of our times."

McLaughlin also noted the strong influence of the spirituality of St. Ignatius in Lynch's emphasis on God's thorough engagement with the world: "He pointed out that faith must have a body; spirituality involves concrete action in time." The book includes sections on the role of the arts in society, images of hope and faith (and how they function with personal and societal woes), a spirituality for public life, the dynamic between the secular and sacred, and new developments in theology.

In 1943, Lynch contributed his own thoughts to a topic that has probably been addressed four billion times since the novel became king: "the vexing problem of the Catholic writer." Is there such a thing? Was there once? Does the Catholic writer have something unique to bring to the world? Unlike some of his successors in this endeavor, Lynch did not argue that there was no such thing, or that all writers sought the same truth, but instead criticized "those who would warn us not to begin to use a Catholic language, who will keep insisting that the vision of the writer is shared alike by all men—regardless of race, color, or creed." Why? Because wrestling with Catholic dogmas and moral teachings was part of what gave Catholic writers their distinct place in the world of letters:

> Now no one has so little sense as to suggest that we must be obnoxious inserters of the Catholic word—

doing all this with a certain vacuous deliberation. Nevertheless, there is something to be said for a deliberate supernatural art. For we have dreadfully exaggerated the necessity of our men of letters writing with a Catholic subconsciousness only (the profession of writing becomes more mysterious every day). But, in reality, it is sharply conceived dogma and the dialectic of the same that makes all the difference in the world.

A comment later in that same essay gives another hint as to why Flannery O'Connor found Lynch such an intriguing thinker. "What a pity if we are led to believe that there can be no writers today until we have educated the people to the point where they will accept the insertion of some sort of realism between the puritanic and the prurient," Lynch wrote. "Oh yes, it is a problem, but let us be grave enough to recognize that it is only a very small part of the problem."

I remember thinking ten years ago the same thought that occurs to me in looking back at William Lynch now: he would have made an incredible novelist.

47

MARY KARR
"Astride the Polarities of Sacredness and Secularity"

"**A**ny way I tell this story is a lie," wrote Mary Karr in the prologue to her 2009 memoir, *Lit*, "so I ask you to disconnect the device in your head that repeats at intervals how ancient and addled I am." On its own, it's an amazing line, but I found it particularly arresting when I first read it in her book when it was released in paperback in 2011. At the time, I was prepping a syllabus for a college course on spiritual memoir, a genre fraught with questions of authority and authenticity (where have you gone, James Frey? A nation turns its lonely eyes to you), and I loved how Karr immediately complicated the suspension of disbelief for every reader.

Lit was Karr's third entry into the genre after *The Liar's Club* (1995) and *Cherry* (2000) and tells the story (among many others) of her recovery from alcoholism and her entrance into the Catholic Church. In a review of *Lit*, Anna Keating compared Karr to St. Augustine—she's not the first to do so, though Karr would scoff at the comparison—but also noted that the book was *not* marketed as a spiritual autobiography.

"Unlike most conversion narratives written by or about people who go on to live extraordinarily holy or influential lives—St. Augustine, Thomas Merton, Dorothy Day— Karr's book reminds us of the remarkable and quiet heroism of ordinary life," Keating wrote. "Getting up every morning, staying sober, working, saying thank you, kneeling in prayer and trying not to scream obscenities at the people we love the most, the people who have failed us and whom we have failed."

Born in Texas in 1955, Karr was a poet long before she was a memoirist. Her poetry collections include *Abacus* (1986), *The Devil's Tour* (1993), *Viper Rum* (1998), *Sinners Welcome* (2006), and *Tropic of Squalor* (2018). The Jesse Truesdell Peck Professor of English Literature at Syracuse University, she has been honored with numerous awards, including the Whiting Writer's Award, a Guggenheim Fellowship, and numerous Pushcart Prizes for her poetry.

Part of Karr's quotidian charm as a memoirist, Keating noted in her review of *Lit*, comes from her habit of not taking herself too seriously. "Like Augustine's before her, Karr's prose often sounds more like poetry. Also like Augustine, Karr is intelligent, well connected and a bit self-conscious to find herself in this ragtag religion," Keating wrote. "She knows what you're thinking. She knows how crazy this all sounds. It used to sound pretty crazy to her as well. That is part of Karr's charm as a narrator. She takes herself lightly, even when dealing with the heaviest of matters."

Karr also once admitted to Terry Gross of National Public Radio that she was wary of herself as a memoirist in general, calling her three books a "low rent form" of the genre— a topic Karr also addressed in *The Art of Memoir*. "It was the province of weirdos and saints and film stars with fake boobs—or you could be a prime minister or something," she said, not that of a writer with a fairly developed case of imposter syndrome.

Karr's self-deprecation and sense of humor come across in a 2019 interview with James Martin, S.J. As a professor, she noted, she often found herself complaining about her students filling up her office hours, especially when "there are very important things that I am thinking I have to do, you know—like get my mascara on and get my nails done." In her daily practice of Ignatian examen, however, she found herself recognizing that whenever a student came in, "even when it was awkward—I noticed God was always there with me." This lead her to double her office hours instead.

Karr also has the ability to puncture some of the pieties that go along with frequently used spiritual phrases or tropes of Ignatian spirituality. "I don't much care to see God in all things," she once wrote. What? *Sacré bleu!* Somewhere St. Ignatius just fainted. In a 2011 interview, she was asked what she meant by it. "I want to find God where I want to find him," she said. "You know, when it's convenient, when I'm ready—like maybe Christmas Eve or Easter, where we've got it kind of taped off."

"In conveying the search for God in the things of this world, Karr walks a careful line—neither devolving into pious pap nor alienating nonreligious readers," Timothy O'Brien, S.J., observed. Though Karr is "acutely aware of a 'certain type of church lady who doesn't like me,' she speaks convincingly of God to believers and nonbelievers alike." She embodies another principle of Ignatian spirituality: she meets people—students, readers, drunks, seekers, and more—where they are. O'Brien writes:

Standing astride the polarities of sacredness and sec-
ularity, she addresses both the pre- and the uncon-
verted at the same time and in the same voice. Her
task, as she sees it, is to write truthfully about the
unavoidably religious world she inhabits, without
alienating those who "don't want to hear about Jesus."

48

WENDELL BERRY
The Cranky Professor-Farmer

Wendell Berry is a person of many labels. Is he a farmer? A novelist? An environmental activist? An essayist? A poet? A cultural critic? A cranky old professor? A Christian prophet? One thing many readers can agree on is that he has been a voice of practical reason and concise cultural commentary in his more than eighty books published over six decades.

My own first encounter with Wendell Berry's writings was not through his poetry or his fiction, but his essays. It came in college, when a philosophy professor assigned *Another Turn of the Crank*, Berry's book of five essays on the global economy, health care, forest preservation, private property, and wealth and ecology. In a 1995 review of the book, Patrick Samway, S.J., wrote that "all of these essays address the mind and heart with the same forcefulness and clarity as the writings of Annie Dillard, Henry David Thoreau, or Wallace Stegner."

To that august list I would add distributists like Peter Maurin and G. K. Chesterton and early Garry Wills (included here mostly so I could write "early Garry Wills"), but at the time my college-student reaction was a simple one:

did Wendell Berry just now leap off the page and hit me over the head with a fencepost?

The writing was lyrical but commonsensical and practical. Berry, who had returned decades before to the farming life of his childhood and was an advocate for time-tested agrarian living, drove home the point that the United States had been built on certain principles—respect for the land, shared small communities and economies, the handing down of tried-and-true traditions and lifestyles, an assumption that a life of faith was a natural one, a management of resources that allowed for seasonal cycles—that were all being abandoned, sacrificed to the gods of technological innovation, individualism, commercialism, and unfettered capitalism.

In my final paper for that class I argued that Berry was right, but his solution was wrong: the only solution was Christian Marxism. (Can it be there was only one year I was twenty-one? It must have been a long one then.) In sharp, practical prose reminiscent of Berry himself, the professor tore my essay apart. But I still remember the book well.

If you ask Berry's many fans, that slim volume isn't usually among their favorites. Berry first made his bones with his poetic works of the 1960s and 1970s, like *The Broken Ground* (1964), and many environmentalists and distributists hold dear his 1977 collection of essays, *The Unsettling of America: Culture and Agriculture*. His novels—the first, *Nathan Coulter,* was published in 1960—have their own fans, and you can usually find them gravitating toward his "Port William novels" like *Hannah Coulter* (2004) or *Jayber Crow* (2000). (Keep your ears peeled next time you're at the farmer's market—one chance in twelve that guy selling you homemade mead named his son Jayber.)

In a 2019 review of *What I Stand On*, a husky two-volume

anthology of Berry's writing edited by Jack Shoemaker, Jon Sweeney identified exactly when he became a Wendell Berry enthusiast: at the age of sixteen. The owner of a bookstore in the suburbs of Chicago that Sweeney haunted as a teenager gave him two of Berry's books, *The Wheel* (a book of poems) and *Recollected Essays,* and said, "I think you should get to know this author." Sweeney did her one better, becoming so obsessed with Berry's writings that he decided a few years later to undertake an impromptu pilgrimage to Berry's farm in Port Royal, Kentucky. Alas, Berry wasn't home, but it didn't dampen Sweeney's enthusiasm for his writings.

"There is always movement in Wendell Berry's sentences. He writes about what he has experienced, what he has learned, and always with humility for what he does not know. The natural world is his primary teacher: its rhythms, its largesse, its mysteries," Sweeney wrote. "And in the essays, the natural world often reflects how change in humans is also natural, inexplicable, and possible. I think this is what many who love his writing appreciate most about Berry, whether they realize it or not. For his Christian readers, this becomes an expansion of what we understand as conversion."

The focus on conversion can seem a bit ironic in Berry's case, because at first glance he doesn't seem to be much of a fan of change in general. "He frequently questions society's attempts to improve things, modernize or make ways of living more efficient. Those words—*improve, modernize, efficient*—might as well be in quotation marks whenever they appear in a Berry essay. He doubts them consistently," Sweeney wrote.

There were moments in the anthology where Berry made Sweeney's hackles rise: "He is not always right. Any essayist worth reading will anger and annoy you from time to time.

Berry can be cranky." On the other hand, "his wisdom, and his call to better habits, is too essential. To ignore Wendell Berry is like trying to ignore your grandmother: You just can't."

Two years before Sweeney's review, Anna Keating wrote a review of Laura Dunn's documentary *Look & See: A Portrait of Wendell Berry*. In the film, an eighty-three-year-old Berry "reads his essays in a Southern drawl over images of his working farm, the land he and his family have cultivated in Kentucky for five generations. He and his wife returned to this land after graduate school, in search of home and sense of place or, as William Faulkner once called it, 'significant soil,'" Keating wrote.

The filmmakers never interview Berry on camera; rather, they try to take viewers into Berry's world: "You hear the sound of footsteps as an unseen person walks through the hills or around the farm. You get to know some of the people Berry loves: his wife and collaborator, Tanya, his daughter, Mary, and his fellow farmers, both industrial, subsistence and organic."

Berry, Keating wrote, "is an advocate of small farms, rural communities, and Judeo-Christian values like kindness, all of which have been harmed by 'get big or get out' industrial agriculture. His life and work bear witness to the fact that it is never Christian to say, 'I can do whatever I want with my own land' or 'my own body.' We are stewards, not owners. What's more, the attitude of 'I can do whatever I want' is toxic to earth and water, family and community."

Keating owns a small business with her husband, and has a particular interest both in Catholic social teaching and in distributist writers, including the aforementioned Chesterton and Maurin but also Hilaire Belloc and Dorothy Day.

She defined distributism as a way of thinking that "seeks to unite what has been separated, labor and capital, through the ownership of small businesses and farms or through the ownership of tools and a trade or through participation in a guild, so that wealth is not consolidated in the hands of a few wealthy individuals (capitalism) or in the hands of the state (socialism)."

The life Wendell Berry has created and the views he espouses, she wrote, "both are in line with this vision and can prove helpful to Catholics, serving as an antidote to the many ills of our time."

49

Phil Klay
Searching for a God of New Life

Phil Klay's 2020 novel, *Missionaries,* gained more than a few impressive accolades in the months after its release. The book was selected by former president Barack Obama in December 2020 as one of his "favorite books of 2020" and was named one of "The 10 Best Books of 2020" by the *Wall Street Journal.* Not bad for a debut novel. Klay wasn't even born until 1983, and so we love him but we sorta hate him for it too.

Klay is a former officer in the U.S. Marine Corps who served in the second Iraq War. He is also what New York Catholics call "a Regis man," meaning he graduated from Regis University in Denver, Colorado. (Kidding, kidding!) Klay won the National Book Award for Fiction for his 2014 collection of short stories, *Redeployment,* and was the 2018 winner of the George W. Hunt, S.J., Prize, co-sponsored by The Catholic Chapel & Center at Yale University and America Media. He currently teaches in the MFA writing program at Fairfield University in Connecticut.

In a review of *Missionaries,* Zac Davis noted that the book forces the reader to ask: "What happens to a world, a nation, a society constantly engaged in forever-war?" Klay, he wrote, "belongs to a chorus of talented veteran-writers who are helping to unravel decades of near-collective indifference to military action around the world. He is also part of a new generation of authors who are putting to rest the overwrought claims about the death of modern Catholic fiction."

"To say that all violence and warfare is connected is not just a foreign policy claim—it is a moral one," Davis wrote. "The work of literature is the same as that of religion in this area: to remind us that we are all our brothers' keepers, and to show what happens when we fail. For a number of the characters in *Missionaries*, their encounters with violence function as a sort of baptism that leaves another kind of indelible mark on their souls." And Klay, Davis noted, seems to draw upon two wellsprings in his meditations on violence:

> God and violence intermingle in the novel in a way that only a writer worthy of claiming a Catholic imagination could accomplish. A staple of the Catholic literary tradition, from St. Paul's description of baptism as death to Flannery O'Connor's gory moments of grace, is that conversion is an act of violence. We are only just beginning to come to grips with the cultural violence that Christian missionaries, sometimes armed only with a Roman Missal and lacking any modern sense of inculturation, waged on Indigenous peoples all over the world. It is hard to know whether Klay's military service or all the time he spent in front of a bloodied, crucified God contributed more to his understanding of violence.

In the address Klay delivered upon receiving the Hunt Prize in 2018, he elaborated on the connection between the violence of the world around us and the life of faith. "Paul tells us 'the Kingdom of God is not in word, but in power.' And, at times, I think I can feel that power around me. Catholicism is not, or should not be, a religion of force. Not of hard mechanical rules, but of stories and paradoxes and enigmatic parables," he wrote.

"It is an invitation to mystery, not mastery, to communion, not control. It is a religion that fits with what I know of reality, that helps me live honestly, and that helps me set aside my dreams of a less atavistic world in which men follow rational orders and never rebel. Perfect obedience, after all, comes not from men, but machines. Fantasies of control are fantasies of ruling over the dead. And my tortured God is not a God of death, but of new life."

In a 2015 interview, Klay discussed *Redeployment*, his collection of short stories, with Kevin Spinale, S.J. One of a number of compelling answers Klay gave in the interview came when Spinale questions him about the connection between being a soldier and being a writer.

Klay spoke of the need every veteran has to find someone or some way to communicate his or her experience of war. "Sin is a lonely thing, a worm wrapped around the soul, shielding it from love, from joy, from communion with fellow men and with God," he said. "The sense that I am alone, that none can hear me, none can understand, that no one answers my cries—it is a sickness over which, to borrow from Bernanos, 'the vast tide of divine love, that sea of living, roaring flame which gave birth to all things, passes vainly.'"

That need for communication, however, can be stymied by a variety of factors. "There's a kind of mysticism about war experience that both soldiers and civilians often buy into. There is a lot of political weight put on how the experience ought to be interpreted and expectations about what that experience is supposed to mean. Sometimes it's painful to discuss," Klay said. "And oftentimes there's an unwillingness among veterans to expose oneself to judgment, which goes hand in hand with a civilian unwillingness to accept complicity in war."

We expect veterans to feel the heavy weight of their actions in war. But why do we never expect civilians to accept our own responsibility for our forever-wars?

50

RON HANSEN
Faith, Ecstasy, and
a Catholic Sensibility

I f you're ever looking for some good Lenten reading—
or just a great book to read—here's a recommendation
I've given many times: pick up Ron Hansen's 1991 novel,
Mariette in Ecstasy. As I was preparing for Lent in 2024,
when Ash Wednesday awkwardly fell on the same date as
Valentine's Day, I was reminded that the church has its own
calendar that doesn't often correspond to that of the secular
culture. Our seasons are marked by Advent and Lent, and
also by the regular celebration of feasts, memorials, holy days
of obligation, and days of penance and fasting. It is a culture
Ron Hansen captured well in *Mariette in Ecstasy,* where the
story is structured around the calendar of saints. Even in the
rural, agricultural setting in which the nuns of *Mariette in
Ecstasy* live (the novel is set in 1906), the passage of time is
not marked by the changing of the weather so much as by the
observance of the liturgical calendar.

Mariette in Ecstasy, the story of a young postulant who
begins to have ecstatic (and sometimes torturous) visions
and shows evidence of the wounds of Christ on her body,

received rave reviews upon its release. In 1992, Elizabeth McDonough, O.P., reviewed *Mariette in Ecstasy*, writing that "Hansen's sparse prose is compelling and actually borders on the poetic." Michiko Kakutani of the *New York Times* called it a "luminous novel that burns a laser-bright picture into the reader's imagination, forcing one to reassess the relationship between madness and divine possession, gullibility and faith, sexual rapture and religious ecstasy." Although the novel devoted considerable space to Roman Catholic beliefs and liturgy, she noted, "one need hardly be familiar with that church's teachings to be moved and amazed by this fable."

A movie version was filmed in 1995—for which Hansen wrote the screenplay—but was not released to the public at the time because the production company, Savoy Pictures, was in financial trouble (and closed its doors in 1997). The Rev. Robert Lauder, reviewing it in 1996 at the time of its expected release, called it an "extremely sensitive and beautifully paced film" and "exciting without stooping to the sensational." The film was shown to the larger public for the first time at the 2019 Camerimage International Film Festival.

I first read the novel as a college student and have returned to it several times over the years—and have taught it in more than a few college seminars. That introduction to Hansen's work led me to his broader corpus of novels, short stories, and essays. Though *Mariette* is his only novel with such an explicitly religious theme and setting (well, maybe *Exiles* as well), Hansen, who was ordained a Catholic deacon in 2007, has regularly explored questions of faith and religious belonging in his writing.

"Because of my Catholicism, I'm pretty sure Catholic themes or attitudes are at least subterranean in whatever I write," Hansen said in a 2014 interview. "And I suspect many Catholic readers who did not know I was a co-religionist would find an affinity for my fiction without being able to put a finger on why. Certain stances and ways of being just leak through in a book." Hansen, who completed the full thirty-day Spiritual Exercises of St. Ignatius Loyola at a Jesuit retreat house in 2007, said in 2017 that St. Ignatius's "meditation on the two standards has influenced most of my novels."

Born in 1947 in Omaha, Nebraska, Hansen attended Creighton University in his hometown and later attended the famous Iowa Writers' Workshop, where one of his instructors was John Irving. His first novel, *Desperadoes*, was published in 1979, with *The Assassination of Jesse James by the Coward Robert Ford* following four years later. In the decades since, he has published everything from a novel for children to a fictionalized account of the shipwreck memorialized by Gerard Manley Hopkins, S.J., in "The Wreck of the Deutschland" to a novel about Hitler's niece and more. His *A Stay against Confusion* is another go-to book for me, a collection of essays on faith and fiction.

Hansen retired recently from his longtime position as the Gerard Manley Hopkins, S.J., Professor in the Arts and Humanities at Santa Clara University (where he earned a master's in spirituality). He has also been writing essays, poems, and book reviews for a number of different journals for more than three decades, with his first contribution being a 1991 review of Muriel Spark's *Symposium*.

A postscript: Several years ago, I had the chance to interview John Irving for *America* at his office in Toronto. Thinking it would provide valuable background for the story (and because, like most writers, I am a very nosy person), I couldn't help but look at what books Irving himself had laid out on his writing table. Among them was a huge compendium of Bob Dylan's song lyrics, a collection of German Christmas stories, Kathleen Winter's novel *Annabel*—and another selection that warmed my heart: Ron Hansen's 2016 novel, *The Kid*.